BRITISH + IRISH
MODERN
NEW HOUSES AND OLD HOUSES MADE NEW

Foreword by Maggie Toy

BRITISH + IRISH MODERN

NEW HOUSES AND OLD HOUSES MADE NEW

Edited by Hannah Jenkins

images Publishing

Published in Australia in 2018 by
The Images Publishing Group Pty Ltd
ABN 89 059 734 431
6 Bastow Place, Mulgrave, Victoria 3170, Australia
Tel: +61 3 9561 5544 Fax: +61 3 9561 4860
books@imagespublishing.com
www.imagespublishing.com

The Images Publishing Group Reference Number: 1397

All renderings, plans, and illustrations have been supplied courtesy of the architect; photography is attributed throughout, unless otherwise noted.

Maps: Sourced from Free Vector Maps (http://freevectormaps.com); modified by Images Publishing.

Pages 6–7: © Tim Crocker, Brackenbury House

Pages 258–9: © Aiden Monaghan Photography, Ballymagarry Road House

Page 260: © Alice Clancy, Hazel Lane Mews

National Library of Australia Cataloguing-in-Publication entry:

Title: British + Irish Modern: New Houses and Old Houses Made New
ISBN: 9781864707533 (hardback)
Subjects: Architecture – Great Britain – Designs and plans.
Architecture, Domestic – Ireland.
Architecture, British.
Architecture, Modern – 21st century.
Architecture, Domestic – Designs and plans.

Art director | Group production manager: Nicole Boehringer
Research contributor: Joe Boschetti
Senior editor: Gina Tsarouhas
Coordinating editor: Hannah Jenkins
Graphic designer: Ryan Marshall

Printed on 140gsm GoldEast Matt Art paper by Everbest Printing Investment Limited, in Hong Kong/China

IMAGES has included on its website a page for special notices in relation to this and our other publications. Please visit www.imagespublishing.com

CONTENTS

FOREWORD by Maggie Toy

Imagine yourself in a calm relaxed haven, a place soothing and tranquil, perhaps coloured, jewelled and with many family memories, and where the space in your mind is possible. Imagine your sense of home – be it sophisticated, open and apparently simple – designed specifically for you and how you choose to interact with the world. This is the utopia achieved by the homes in this clever collection of both new and renewed properties.

The house can be the most difficult architectural challenge to complete with satisfaction to all, obviously it is a very personal project, the designer has to really understand what the client needs and be able to interpret and enhance those requirements. History is littered with examples where architects were criticised for not getting this right. But what we remember more are the occasions where the designer achieved the perfect balance.

Great demands are made of some homes – Gaston Bachelard thought that 'the house is an instrument with which to confront the cosmos' this certainly could be said of Konstantin Melnikov for example after he was prevented from practising as an architect. He was only able to exude his creative juices out on his own house. The resulting home was genius marrying curves with diamonds in spectacular style.

By a determination to create an aesthetic that made use of the qualities of iron to the full Victor Horta began his style of curvaceous organic forms that were to become his hallmark. His house in Brussels entices you in with only little clues from the front elevation to what might be behind. Once inside the sinuous forms are witnessed swirling through the building effortlessly lifting the occupier up and around the home. 'My house is my refuge, an emotional piece of architecture, not a cold piece of convenience' said Luis Barragan and he left many clients with environments that fitted their brief, mixing clean lines with bright colours and especially when injected with water something magical. When faced with a site that many thought impossible to build upon because of its steep slope, John Lautner came up with an ingenious solution to provide his clients with a home. In the Chemosphere he piled a central supporting column off which the entire house could 'rotate' just gently touching the slope at the top to allow access.

Sometimes those challenges which we think are insurmountable are the very triggers we need for inventive genius.

The Modernism of today is democratic, eclectic; not obsessed with rules and design strictures, it is open to colour, curve and texture. Each of the examples in this compendium show great skill in the juxtaposition of textures, shapes, and volumes to create a series of inspiration spaces that instil a perfect balance of relaxation, style, sophistication. Importantly, aside from their commitment to the intricate process between designer and client, the architects featured in this book also possess a visionary finesse that aligns with the design philosophies of their predecessors. Sir Edwin Lutyens, for example, in the spirit of adhering to the requirements of his time, was a master of adapting the traditional to the contemporary in this region. This same commitment to honouring the historical within modern architectural realms is reflected in the work of Marta Nowicka, founder of DOM stay and live, who brought a 1950s St John Ambulance station into 21st-century functionality, whilst thoughtfully retaining its historical essence, and 2020 Architects, whose highly acclaimed project, Ballymagarry Road House, conserves the character of historic Irish vernacular whilst beautifully fusing it with modern design concepts.

David Chipperfield once said, 'You don't restore *The Last Supper* by filling in the missing bits – you preserve. You accept the material that has somehow survived'.

The houses here are open to experimentation with form and material, but they are also selected for levels of comfort, dramatic expression of traditional and contemporary architecture, as well as houses that capitalise on longer and warmer summers imposed by changing weather patterns in this corner of the globe. The houses here are designed with indoor spaces and intimate courtyards for play and recreation that draw in light and shield from the extreme weather elements yet maintain an eye on sustainability and affordability.

And so with the notions of present and the future, the architects in this book carry the mantle of designing the perfect home. The constant battle between architect, client and planner to create architecture that achieves these conflicting aspirations is hard fought and rarely won. But across the pages of this book innovative architects demonstrate how to bring individual and contemporary notions of 'home' to fruition, and which gives us a strong sense of the region's dazzling architectural future.

Sandy Rendel Architects

142 SOUTH STREET

The brief for this project was to create a sustainable and contemporary family home that made the most of a dramatic but constrained brownfield site. Located on the banks of the River Ouse in Lewes, the site historically functioned as a wharf for the old quarry/cement works behind.

The house occupies a prominent position overlooking the river and nature reserve floodplain beyond, and is set against a backdrop of chalk cliffs to the south. The project aim was to design a unique home that respected its history and surroundings through form and material choice.

The main body of the house is a simple two-storey pitched roof structure. It is reminiscent of the adjoining buildings but has a ridgeline that has been carved away to break down the building's scale and reflect the contours of the cliff face behind. In addition, the simple plan arrangement has been subtly distorted at each end to draw in key views and provide a covered terrace protected from the weather and buffered from the sound of the adjacent road.

A simple palette of self-finished materials was used to emphasise the buildings form. Each was carefully chosen to be robust, weather naturally, develop character, and reflect the tonal and material qualities of the site and surrounds.

On the ground floor an exposed frame has been constructed from board-marked concrete to reflect the tone and texture of the rugged concrete river wall below. Walls built from handmade glazed Sussex brickwork – a material traditional to the town – face South Street. This gives the home a softer texture and more intimate scale.

Above the muted tones of this masonry base, the first-floor walls and roofs are wrapped in a homogenous rain-screen skin that articulates the form of the upper volume. For this, the architects used a Corten steel expanded mesh, which weathers naturally into a striking red/ochre colour. This echoes the local red clay brickwork and tiles, whilst remaining distinct and alluding to the site's industrial heritage.

Traditional architectural elements such as gutters and eaves have been removed or concealed behind the mesh rain screen. This allows for crisp and clean detailing of the continuous surface and emphasises the home's primary form.

PROJECT SPECIFICATIONS

Location: Lewes, East Sussex, England

Area: 257 m² (2766 ft²)

Completed: 2015

Photography: Richard Chivers (pages 11, 12, 13 bottom, 15); Oliver Perrott (page 13 top)

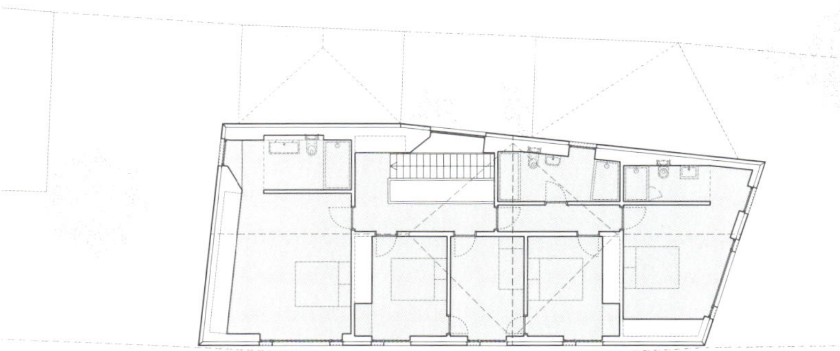

First-floor plan

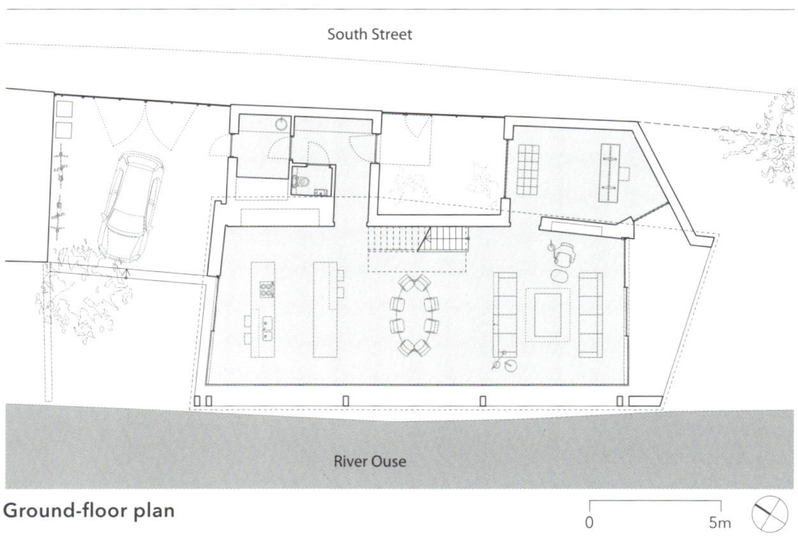

Ground-floor plan

Ansty Plum is a home and studio in rural Wiltshire that has undergone an impressive retrofit and bold studio extension.

Comprising two imaginative buildings commissioned in the 1960s and 70s, the first is a one-bedroom house designed by David Levitt and the second, a studio and garage designed by the Smithsons.

The intensive repair, upgrading and re-organising of the two buildings brought about an 80 percent reduction in their energy use. The buildings are radically sited on a steep wooded hillside and overlook a collection of historic buildings.

Coppin Dockray Architects

ANSTY PLUM HOUSE + STUDIO

The brick and timber house has a simple open plan with a rectangular, singular-plane roof following the gradient of the land. The stone and concrete studio, hedged into the slope, peeps onto an ancient woodland track.

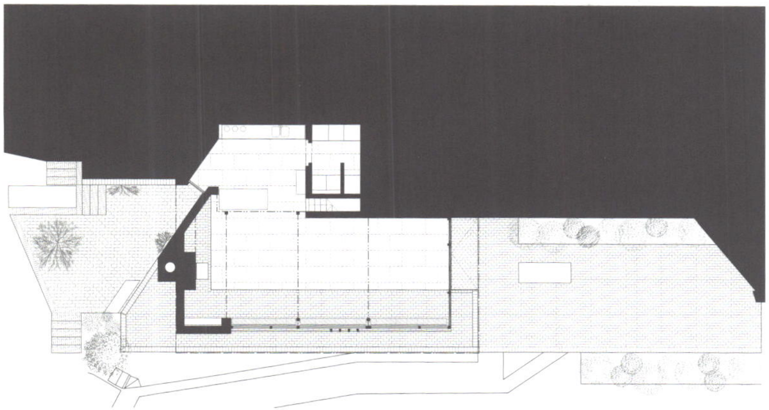

Lower-floor plan

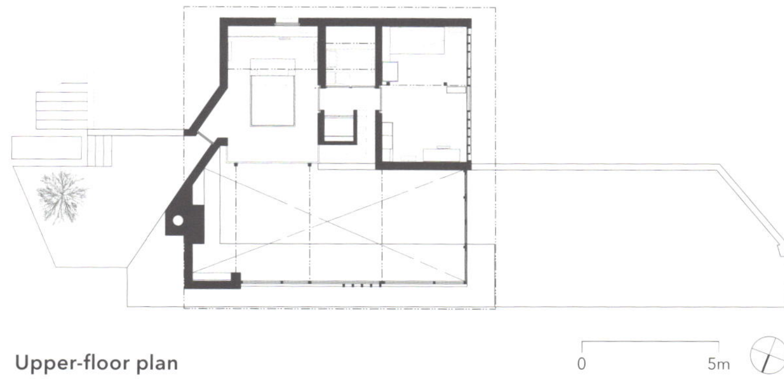

Upper-floor plan

A number of changes had been made to the house over the decades, whilst the studio, after suffering structural failure, water ingress and decay, had been left derelict. Many accretive changes were removed to express the architectural qualities of the original house. The architects opened up the main space by removing a late addition bathroom and internal walls. They then created a new bedroom and study, and added central heating systems. As a result, the home once again displays clarity of intent and can be comfortably occupied throughout the year.

The architects also brought the studio back into use. The failed roof was replaced with an insulated zinc roof and cast-concrete copings. The structure was underpinned, tanked and insulated. Services and heating were also introduced. The studio now glows a warm pink colour from the meticulously detailed Douglas fir lining and joinery. The original structure was extended and hedged into the hill, creating a moody concrete and stone washroom that looks into a bank of prolific ferns. Access to the Smithsons' original working drawings allowed the architects to interpret many of the zinc, stone and timber details. This enabled the creation of a seamless extension that preserves the spirit of the building without compromising its functionality.

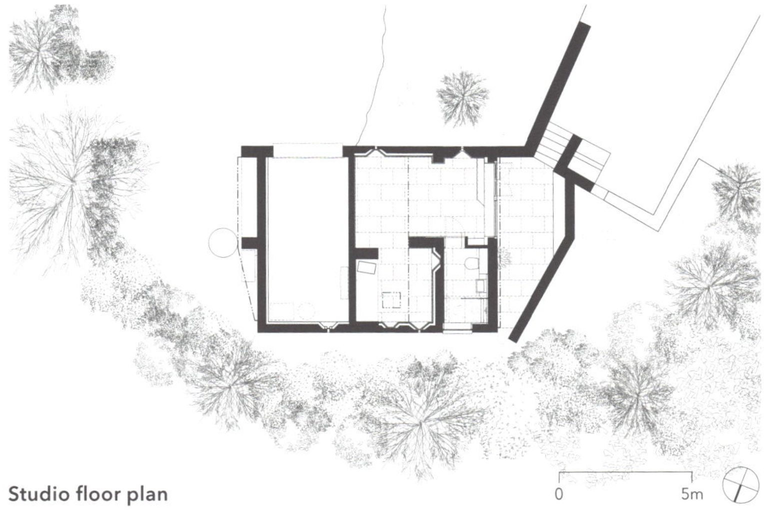

Studio floor plan

PROJECT SPECIFICATIONS

Location: Wiltshire, England

Area: 150 m² (1615 ft²)

Completed: 2015

Photography: Brotherton Lock

Located in the centre of Castleton in the Peak District National Park, Artemis Barn was in continuous agricultural use for over 250 years before falling derelict in the 1990s. The owner wanted to celebrate the barn's existing qualities whilst converting it into an exciting new home.

The main challenge was working with both the constraints and opportunities of the original building. Peak District National Park planning restrictions also gave very limited scope for new openings, particularly to the north wall, which is a long and blank façade.

Chiles Evans + Care Architects

ARTEMIS BARN

The new plan challenges the idea of home: a living room without a view, a principal bedroom next to the main entrance and spaces for eating and relaxing defined within the openness of the existing volume. The materials reinforce the agricultural past of the building and a new reclaimed-stone roof punctured by a large light restores the original building's mass and drops light into the heart of the space.

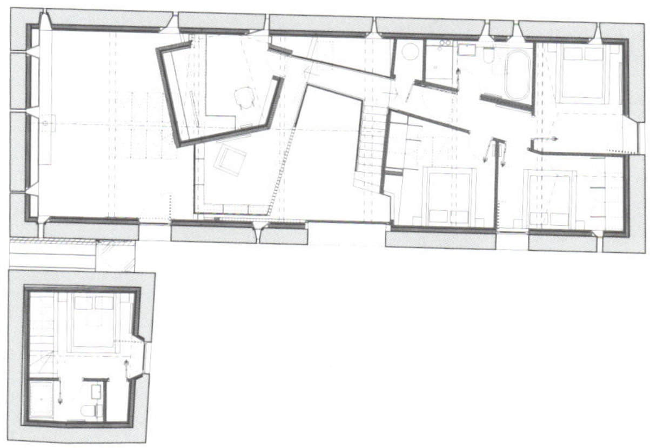

First-floor plan

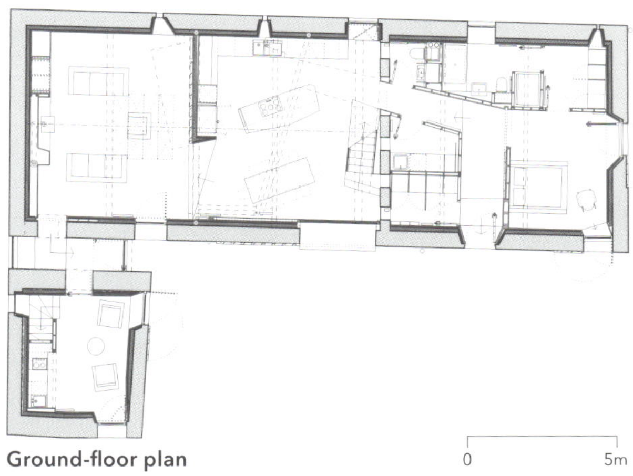

Ground-floor plan

The original rolling timber barn door has been minimally refurbished so when closed the barn retains its original appearance. It is a frameless glazed link to a small cottage that gives the structure's underlying modernity away. Internally, timber has been used in both rough and refined finishes. Concrete and steel are left in a raw state, and stone is exposed. The expressive, simple palette of materials reflects the skill of the local craftsmen who have worked on the project.

PROJECT SPECIFICATIONS

Location: Castleton, Peak District National Park, England
Area: 302 m^2 (3251 ft^2)
Completed: 2016
Photography: Phillipa Evans (pages 23, 25, 26); Jen Langfield (pages 24, 27)

The house is at once intimate and vast with new spaces inserted into the major volume, each distinguished through form and material. The kitchen is flooded with light from an enormous glazed sliding door and the staircase is open and structural. Ever-changing daylight is animated throughout the structure, capturing the seasons through new and existing windows. At the first floor, the former hayloft level has three new bedrooms and a bathroom, whilst the space below houses a mixture of utility rooms as well as a single en suite and ground-floor bedroom.

Adam Knibb Architects

AUSTEN HOUSE

This recently converted dwelling is situated on the site of the old St Swithun's School located along North Walls in Winchester. Vacated in 1929, the school had out grown the city centre location allowing the premises to be taken over by a library, followed by further development into residential dwellings. Austen House forms part of this old development.

The clients loved the location but wanted more natural light, a south-facing aspect and additional space. It was conceived that with an access way beside the property, which would only have to provide a right of passage for cars very occasionally, it was possible to build out and create a new room over the top of this space. The client undertook all necessary legal proceedings for permission of a flying freehold, whilst the architects created a very contemporary solution.

The home is located within the town centre conservation area, which meant its architectural addition had to stand out from the main building in both materiality and design.

First-floor plan

A floating timber box lightly touches the building via glass-slot windows and cantilevers out over the access way, providing dramatic internal space and making it a prominent feature down North Walls Road. Vertical timber cladding and large sections of glass have been specifically designed to give a greater feeling of verticality and sense of place. A sky lantern linked with actuator-controlled ventilation provides the space with additional aspects to the sky. The box stands delicately on two galvanised steel columns at the extent of the boundary.

The nature of the site meant principles of construction also had to be considered. The project was partially completed off-site to ensure minimal disruption on site.

PROJECT SPECIFICATIONS

Location: Winchester, Hampshire, England
Area: 21 m^2 (226 ft^2)
Completed: 2015
Photography: Martin Gardner

Platform 5 Architects

BACKWATER

This new detached home replaces an outdated bungalow on a promontory in a secluded lagoon in the Norfolk Broads. Designing a new building for the plot provided an opportunity to enhance the setting by establishing a stylish counterpoint to more traditionally designed neighbouring houses, whilst respecting the peaceful location. A key objective was to create simple, contemporary living spaces orientated to take advantage of surrounding views.

The house is arranged as three low-rise bays, each with pitched roofs echoing the working boat sheds typically found on the broads. Each bay has been positioned to address the waterfront, optimising natural light and providing internal living spaces with framed views across the water. The home's entrance is relatively low-key, with the main architectural drama reserved for the waterside elevation. Timber cladding offers a strong material contrast with neighbouring houses and is already beginning to weather back attractively, providing a sympathetic presence against the surrounding trees and water. Deep eaves emphasise the home's bold contemporary silhouette and provide sheltered external spaces, which are useable across the seasons. Externally, a layered timber landscape provides the transition from water level up to the elevated ground floor.

Inside, a simple broken-plan arrangement accommodates family life and allows for flexible living. The central bay contains a large kitchen and dining area, which flows into the adjacent double-height living and relaxation space. Bedrooms occupy the third bay and are connected by an impressive spiral staircase, which rises from the entrance hallway. Each space has a carefully considered interior with built-in furniture.

The peninsula location made construction a difficult task. In response, the project was designed with easily transportable, lightweight elements. Backwater is a highly sustainable family home, which brings a strong architectural presence to a sensitive waterside setting.

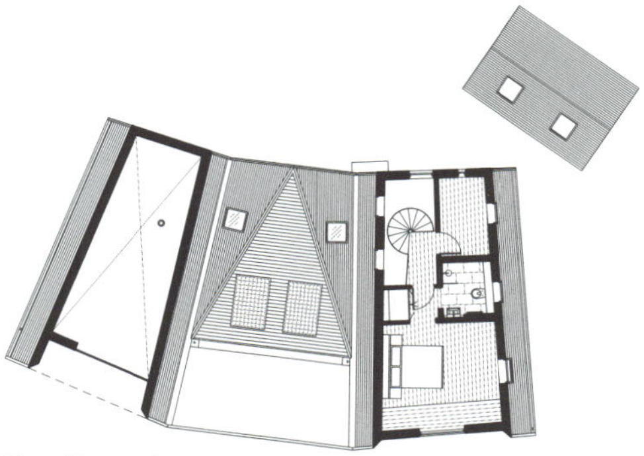

First-floor plan

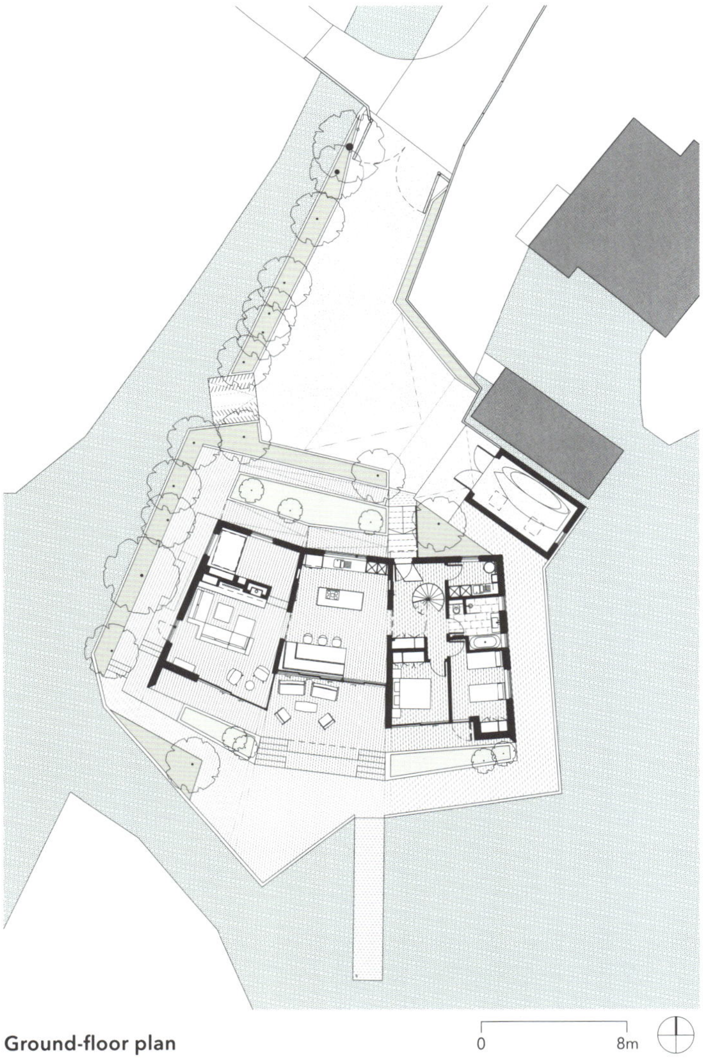

Ground-floor plan

PROJECT SPECIFICATIONS

Location: Norfolk, England
Area: House: 165 m^2 (1776 ft^2); Boathouse: 20 m^2 (215 ft^2)
Completed: 2016
Photography: Alan Williams

2020 Architects

BALLYMAGARRY ROAD HOUSE

The concept behind this home was to rebuild and conserve an existing dwelling and old forge whilst creating a visual barrier for a modern, highly glazed, curved-roof living extension to sit on the block behind.

Two gables create strong basic shapes and replicate the agricultural buildings throughout the Irish countryside. The architects and planners wanted to retain as much of the original forge as possible and conserve its character, which would help to ground the design in the Irish vernacular. The curved roof allows the extension to sit lower than the original forge and addresses the need for two storeys. The two strong forms are divided by a flat-roofed section, which has been planted as a wildflower meadow. Due to the sloping nature of the site, the building increases in height along the road from west to east. This is an original feature used to enhance the drama of design internally.

The home is approached from the lower western gable. Upon entering, a 16-metre-long (52-foot-long) wall of natural unpainted stone pulls views into the depth of the house. Partially rebuilt using the original stone, this thick wall ties the modern structure to the site's history. The wall increases in scale when moving down a corridor created by the two competing building forms and wildflower roof above. The tension between these two spaces sets up much of the home's drama: the curving wall of the modern extension pushes against the heft of a massive stone element. To ensure its integration into the undulating fields beyond, the home sits on seven different levels.

The project incorporates a glulam-engineered superstructure consisting of five curved beams, which have been left exposed, making it one of the home's most prominent features. The beams break up the long cylindrical ceiling and provide a natural beauty and warmth to a largely blank canvas. Lowering environmental impact was also of great importance during the build and sourcing a locally made timber structure, as opposed to a steel structure or imported timber frame, was essential.

This home demonstrates the flexibility of design timber can provide. It is a project that uses structure not only as a means by which to support a roof and walls, but as an integrated component of the overall design aesthetic.

PROJECT SPECIFICATIONS

Location: Portrush, Northern Ireland
Area: 280 m^2 (3014 ft^2)
Completed: 2015
Photography: Aiden Monaghan Photography

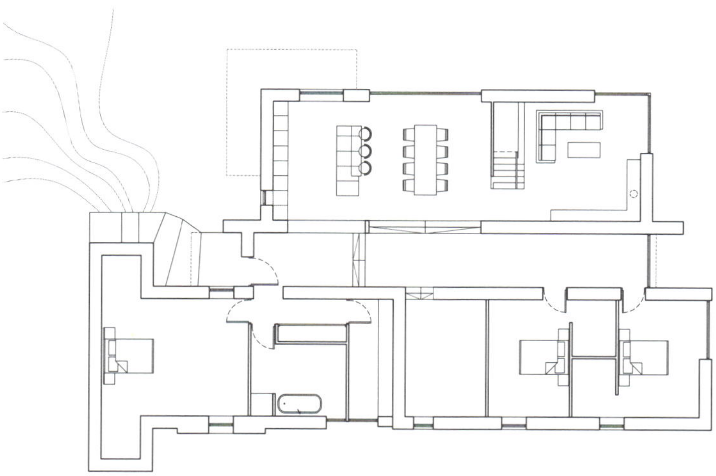

Ground-floor plan

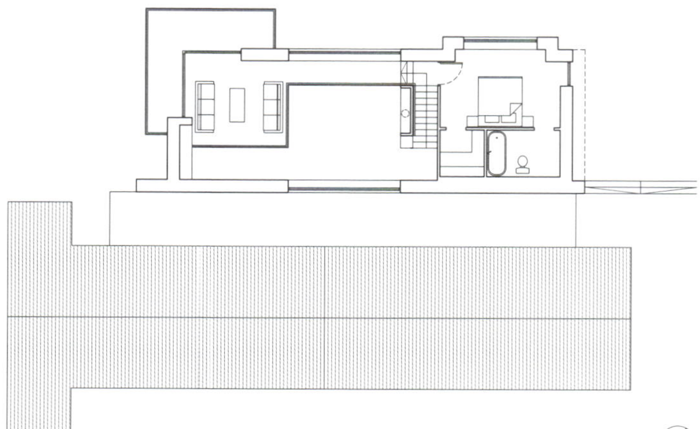

First-floor plan

Adam Knibb Architects

BECKETT HOUSE

Tight planning constraints meant the architects had to take an inventive view towards attaining the space required for this whole-house refurbishment and extension. The original home's countryside location required the new design to make use of a planning loophole that only allowed a small dwelling to be extended by 25 percent if below 120 square metres (1291 square feet).

It was proposed that the existing 1950s farm worker cottage would be refurbished into a very contemporary house. The ground-floor extension gives the opportunity for a large vista view to the garden and woodlands beyond. At first-floor level a new master suite was added, which pokes out around the existing building and benefits from dual aspect views. The exterior concept was for a distinct datum between the ground and first floor – a solid monolithic masonry base at the ground and a first-floor timber box appearing to sit lightly on top. To avoid an overbearing presence from the road, the design takes a soft and modern approach at the home's front then completely transforms at the rear.

Internally, a radical floating staircase allows natural light to flow through the front hallway and into the rear open-plan space. Large slim-line sliding doors blur the transition between internal and external space.

PROJECT SPECIFICATIONS

Location: Crawley, West Sussex, England
Area: 198 m^2 (2131 ft^2)
Completed: 2015
Photography: Martin Gardner

First-floor plan

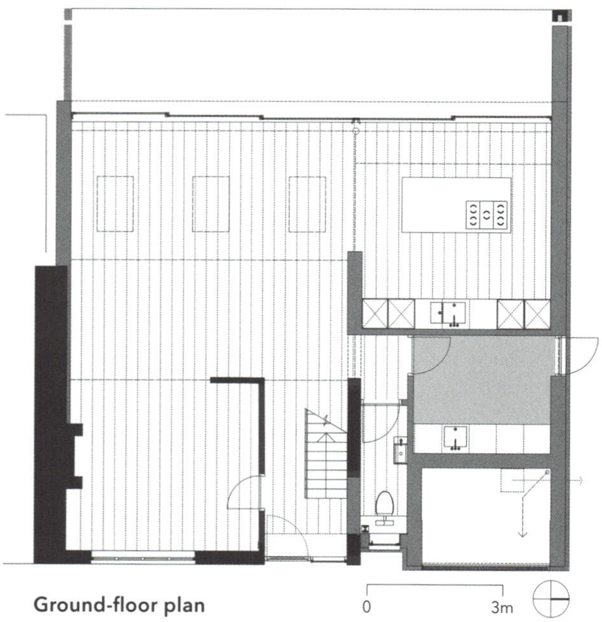

Ground-floor plan

This remodel and extension was designed for a young family with one child. The home forms part of a terrace of five Lillian Villas built in 1879.

The clients wanted a natural, earthy palette of materials and to retain as much of the existing building's fabric as possible, reusing what could not be preserved in the new reconfiguration They also wanted the house to feel connected to the outdoors by framing views to the garden and accommodating for as much natural light as possible. An open plan and sustainability were also important design factors.

Neil Dusheiko Architects

BRACKENBURY HOUSE

The design added a new basement and rear extension to the home, providing an expanded living and kitchen area; sky lit, sun-filled bathrooms; and a home cinema, playroom and guest bedroom. A contemporary rethinking of the basement typology ensured it would be light filled and multifunctional. The space acts as both a playroom for their young son and sophisticated cinema room.

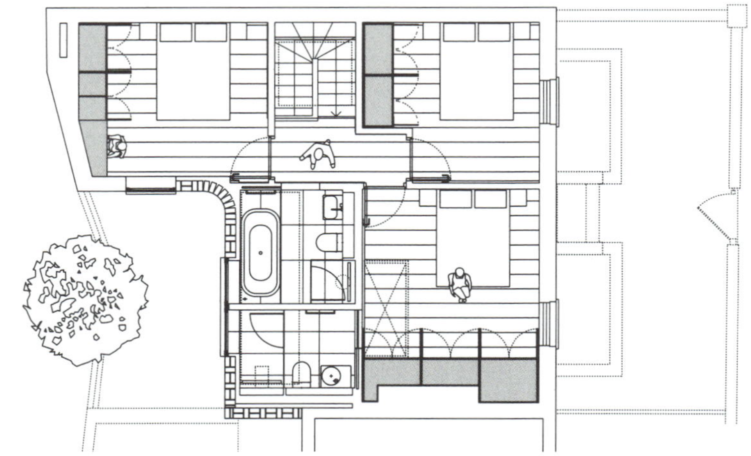

First-floor plan

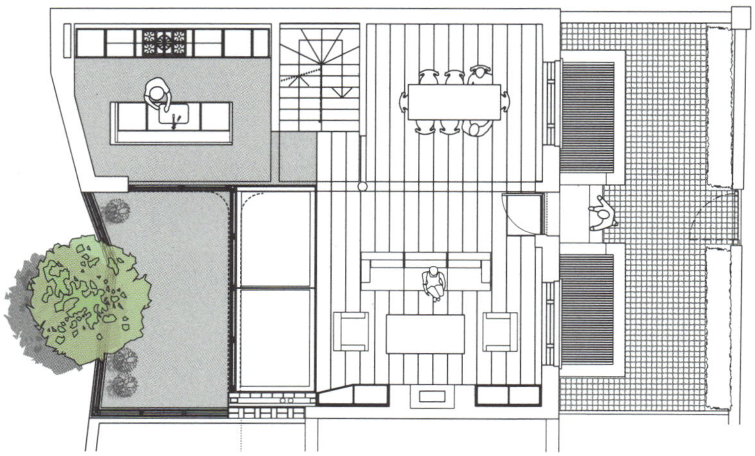

Ground-floor plan

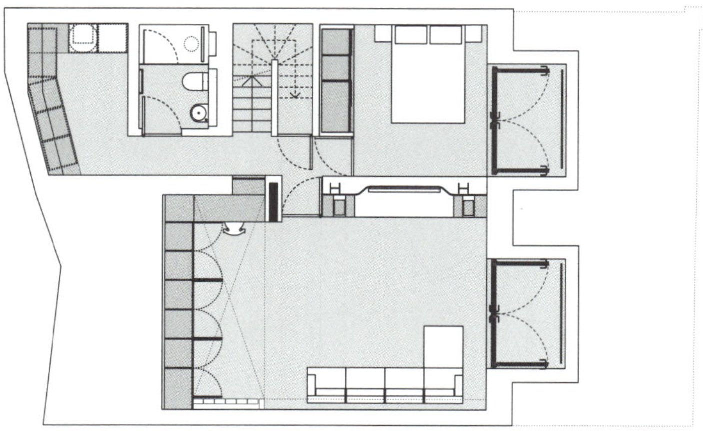

Basement floor plan

0 3m

A carefully selected, unified material palette creates calm and atmospheric spaces, stitching modern design into the historic context of the home's interior. Inherent relationships between re-used materials juxtaposed with modern industrial elements create a sense of aesthetic harmony throughout.

All levels of the home have been opened up to allow existing rooms to give way to an open-plan interior on the ground floor. In the new basement area, large skylights have been cut into the floors above to light the space. The kitchen and living rooms open out to a southwest-facing patio, creating a strong connection between house and garden.

PROJECT SPECIFICATIONS

Location: London, England

Area: 180 m^2 (1938 ft^2)

Completed: 2015

Photography: Tim Crocker (pages 55, 56, 57 right, 58); Agnese Sanvito (pages 57 left, 59 bottom); Charles Hosea (page 59 top)

This award-winning two-bedroom house is arranged around a series of courtyards within the walls of an infill site in East London. The challenge with the L-shaped plot was to create a private house without compromising the neighbour's daylight or privacy.

Four distinct courtyards provide the main source of daylight for the house and open up sightlines through the property, creating functional outdoor spaces. The home's roof is at its lowest point at the rear of the neighbouring property. This sunken-roof design aspect minimises the home's impact within its surrounding context.

Dallas-Pierce-Quintero

COURTYARD HOUSE

The client wanted a home that would make best use of the site whilst allowing for flexible use of space. The result is an almost entirely open plan with separation and variety created with level changes and varying ceiling heights. A standalone study sits opposite the house. Within the space between, there is a walled kitchen garden, which provides the home with a green space, biodiversity, fruit, herbs, and flowers. The second bedroom is located on the ground floor as an extension of the living space and has been subdivided with a curtain. A rear patio provides a quiet space for entertaining and contemplation.

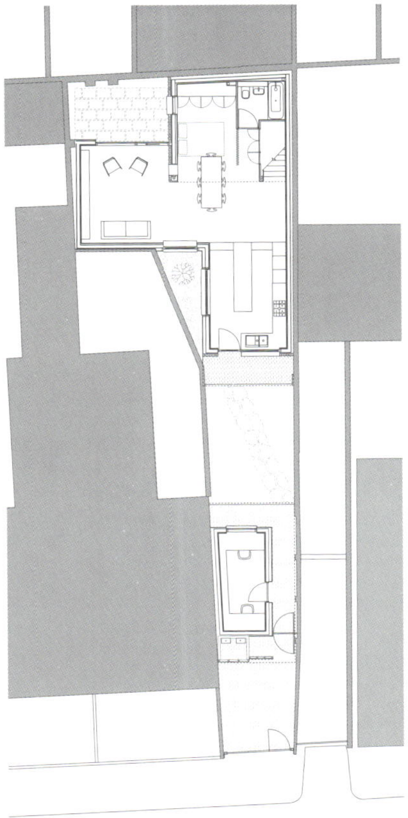

Ground-floor plan

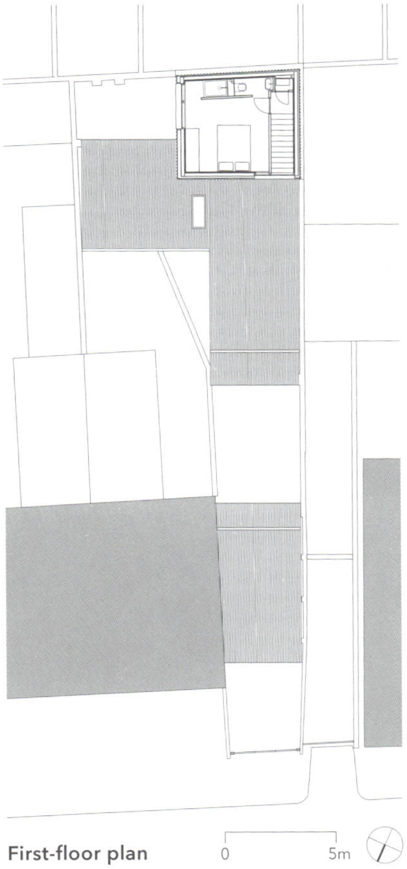

First-floor plan

Timber has been used for the home's structure and chosen for its cost, speed of construction and sustainability. Wall panels were fabricated off site and the roof structure built on site. Internally, the ceiling joists are exposed in the living areas to maximise height and add richness, changing direction as the plan kinks. A visible fire-rated board forms the underside of the ceiling.

The building's materials were chosen for their affordability and resonance with the site. Black-profiled cement sheets have been used to clad the first-floor bedroom and roofs, echoing the corrugated steel on nearby outbuildings, whilst at ground floor, where the majority of the timber walls are protected by the existing brick boundary walls, the exposed walls are faced in blue brick or white render. Below waist height, sawtooth bricks have been used, softening the appearance of the brickwork.

PROJECT SPECIFICATIONS

Location: London, England

Area: 95 m^2 (1023 ft^2)

Completed: 2014

Photography: David Butler (pages 61, 63 right); Rachael Smith (pages 62, 63 top left, 65); Tom Gildon (page 64)

Ashton Porter Architects

DRAG AND DROP HOUSE

In response to a sloping plot, this project has been designed with a two-storey elevation to the rear and a stepped three-storey elevation at the front. The rear of the house has been embedded into the plot and a series of gabion walls provide a transition from the landscape into the main living spaces. These spaces are split into two main areas: kitchen/informal seating and formal living space. The stepping of the site continues through the central circulation space and exits through the front entrance, continuing out into the landscape.

A central circulation core, which connects all three storeys with an open and vertical void, divides the living spaces and sets up a series of rotating views throughout the home, some of which extend out into the plot and frame elements of the landscape.

823 YUR

By cutting into the sloping ground a lower-ground floor level was created, which acts as a retaining structure repeated as an artificial edge at the front elevation. This newly articulated retaining wall wraps into the landscape and acts as a mediator between the ground plane and the main floating volumes of the house above.

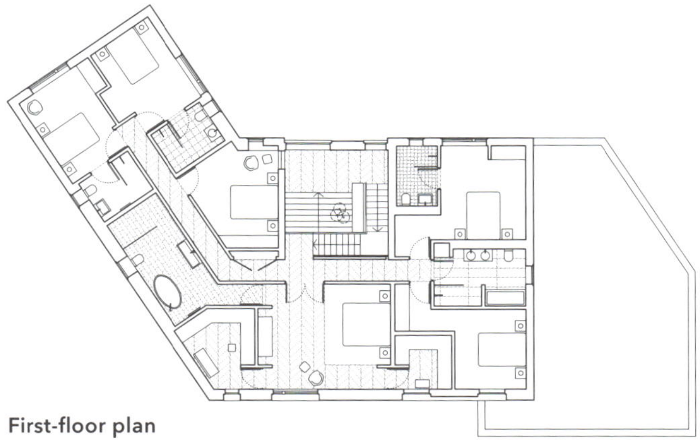

First-floor plan

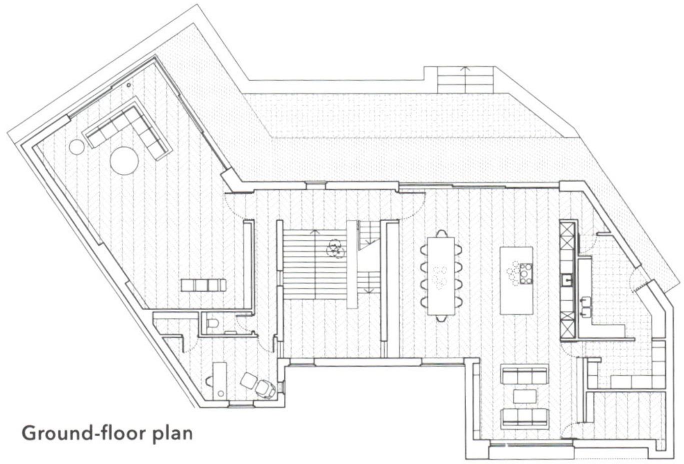

Ground-floor plan

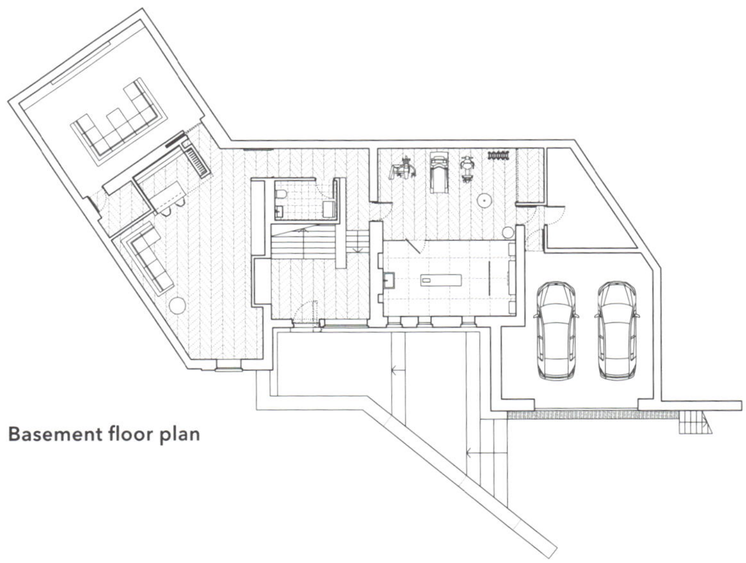

Basement floor plan

PROJECT SPECIFICATIONS

Location: North London, England
Area: 700 m^2 (7535 ft^2)
Completed: 2016
Photography: Andy Stagg

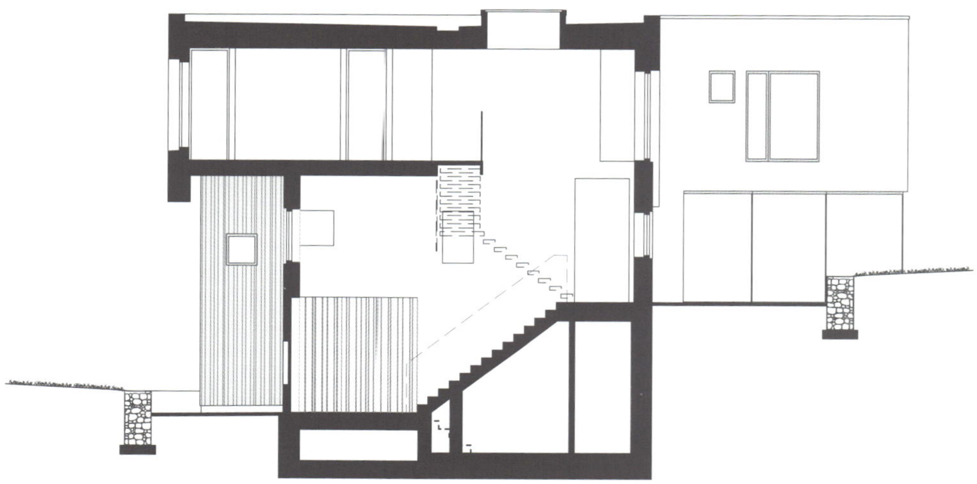

West section

A Small Studio

ESCAPE TO THE ROOF

This residential loft conversion of an Edwardian house includes a refuge for the parents of a growing family. The project brief was to design a place of peace and tranquility they could escape to after a long day's work.

The original four-bedroom family house had an ornate period front and a rear elevation with an apex-shaped closet extension. The aim of the new project was to re-create the apex geometry by making three careful incisions into the roof and inserting simple, modern and beautiful dormers to accentuate the Victorian geometry but in entirely different materials and using modern technology.

The dormers are only 250 millimetres (9.85 inches) apart, so the construction was challenging and required meticulous contractors. The dormers have full-height glazing finished in an apex shape and are framed in a black powder-coated aluminium trim. The dormer sides and roof are clad in vertical-pleated zinc.

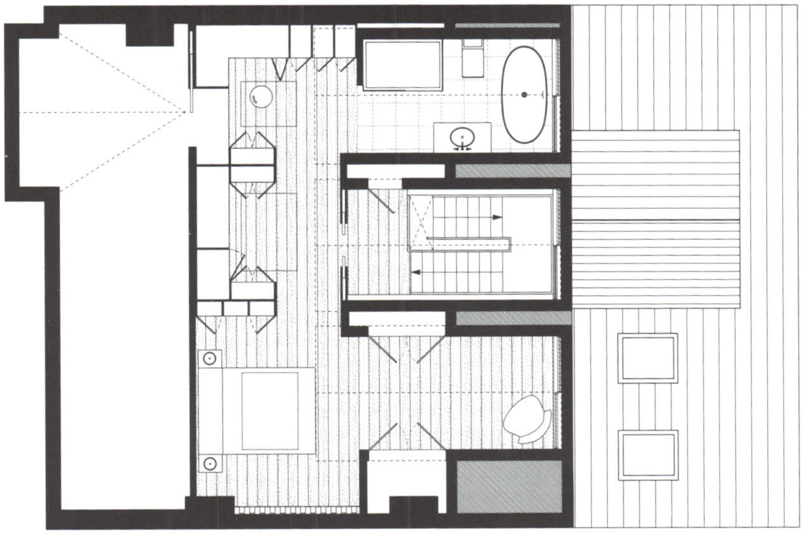

Loft floor plan

Internally, these windows frame views over southeast London and provide a busy backdrop to an otherwise minimal interior. The three spaces (bedroom, bathroom, wardrobe) were kept open-plan throughout the loft and have only been divided using a bespoke joinery system designed by the architect.

PROJECT SPECIFICATIONS

Location: South London, England
Area: 60 m² (646 ft²)
Completed: 2016
Photography: Jim Stephenson

Space and light were critical in the design. In order to maximise natural daylight throughout the house, a central void was cut through the entire structure. The new void has an apex ceiling construction and houses a new freestanding solid oak staircase, which lands gently on the first floor of the original house, respecting its period features.

The focal point of this project is a pleated roof at the back of house. It appears to be formed from a flat surface and forced to crinkle up into a faceted structure as it's pushed up against the exterior wall. From the garden, the pleats are purposefully sunk from view, creating the impression of a simple flat roof, which allows the character of the original building to stand out. The design intention was to evoke a graphic feel within a modern extension, creating a feeling of motion that would emphasise the meeting of old and new.

Bureau de Change

FOLDS HOUSE

The poise of the roof offers natural points of placement for generous skylights. This creates light within the living area and satisfies the owners' desire to see the nearby woodland whilst relaxing in the space.

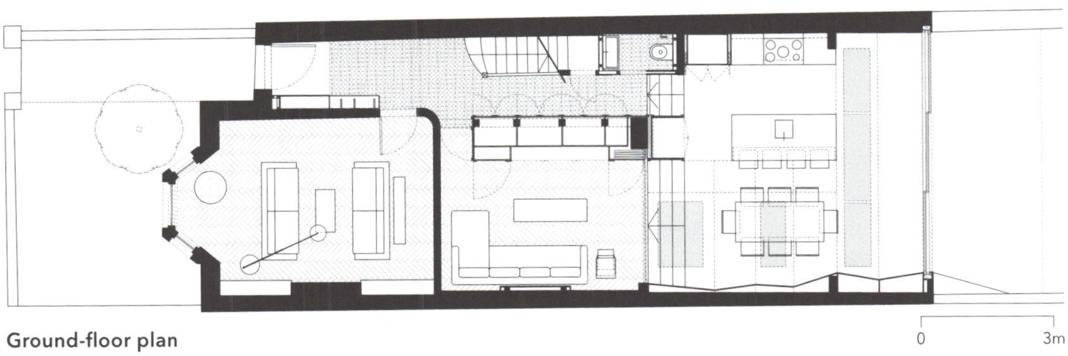

Ground-floor plan

Forming a side and rear extension, the roof expands the existing kitchen and creates a new dining and work area. The end of the pleated ceiling, which is capped by a midnight blue surface that emphasises its ample peaks and troughs, marks the boundary of the kitchen assertively. Darkened surfaces continue through the kitchen into a long passage that extends down the left side of the property, conveniently and discreetly creating a storage and utilities zone.

PROJECT SPECIFICATIONS

Location: North London, England
Area: 40 m^2 (431 ft^2)
Completed: 2015
Photography: Bureau de Change

The home's scheme is characterised by a rich palette of colours, materials and textures, which create a different experience in each space and mark transitions between living spaces. Large terrazzo slabs, encaustic tiles and tonal parquet complement the complexion of the original building, whilst enhancing the graphic impact of the angular extension.

This project design added a light-filled side extension at ground-floor level and a new loft bedroom and bathroom in previously unused roof space to a home in need of modernisation.

By opening up the front and rear reception rooms an open-plan living space was created, providing ample display space for the owner's extensive art collection. A fully glazed skylight to the side extension allows for increased light levels and improved connections between spaces linking the front of the house to the rear garden.

Neil Dusheiko Architects

GALLERY HOUSE

A set of new stairs run full width across the structure, marking the connection between the new and old rooms. Niches have been carved into the depth of the walls to allow for storage and spaces for sculptures to be displayed.

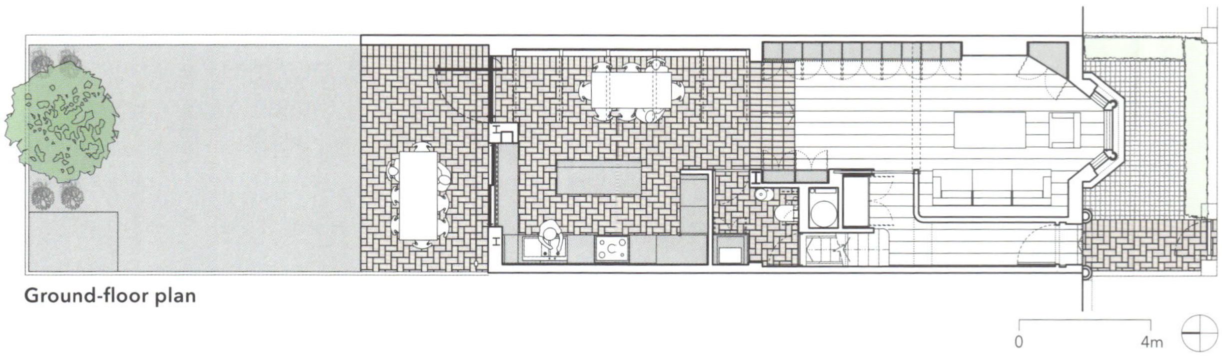

Ground-floor plan

A calm material palette of reclaimed bricks and oak flooring gives a sense of warmth and texture to the home. The rich detailing gives a tactile scale to the new domestic spaces. Built-in kitchen seating provides and informal gathering space that looks out into the garden. A large glass-pivoting door enables generous access to the same outdoor space.

A framework of oak shelving and timber rafters gives structure to the new ground-floor space, providing further display space for art, ceramics and glassware pieces under a bright sun-filled, fully glazed skylight.

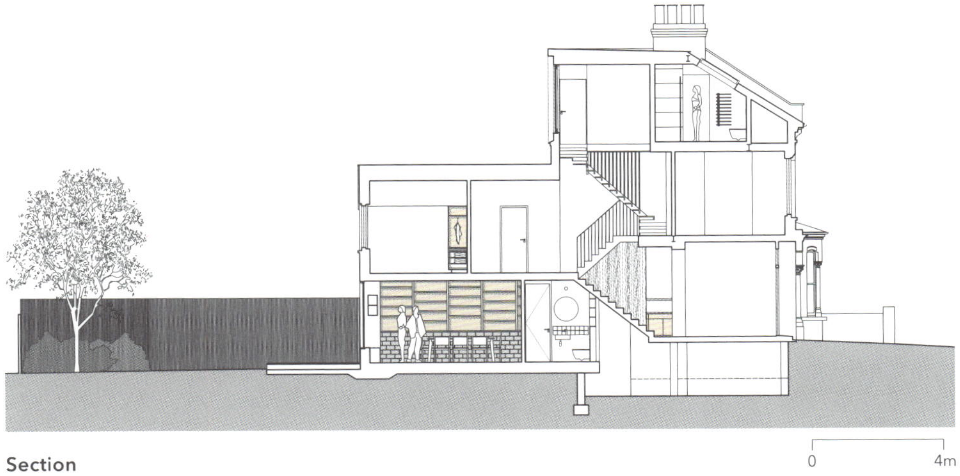

Section

The new loft level is a timber framed zinc-clad structure, which adds an additional bedroom and bathroom to the property. It also allows for panoramic views towards Clissold Park and the distant church steeple.

PROJECT SPECIFICATIONS

Location: London, England

Area: 140 m^2 (1507 ft^2)

Completed: 2016

Photography: Agnese Sanvito (page 85); Tim Crocker (pages 86, 87, 88, 89, 90, 91)

Ström Architects

HARTROW

Hartrow is a large-scale refurbishment and extension project of a 1960s house in Winchester. The original house was unusual in its residential street setting, presenting an entirely different aesthetic, orientation and layout to its neighbours. Part of the challenge was to ensure that the new design would celebrate its mid-century styling whilst bringing its function and performance up to 21st-century standards.

The house was split over several levels to suit the sloping site, with a drive and entrance hall to the street. Externally, the driveway ran steeply alongside the house to the carport at the rear, several levels below. The living rooms and kitchen were located on the top floor. This arrangement of space no longer worked for modern life and the multiple levels felt disconnected from one another and the site.

The new internal layout was arranged to fulfill the needs of a busy modern family. The unused carport was enclosed with sliding glazing and turned into a family room for cooking, playing, eating, and relaxing. This created a relationship with the exterior, allowing the space to open up to the garden for summertime entertaining and supervised play space for the children. A calmer, more sophisticated living room is located on the top floor, taking advantage of views and providing a break from the informal family space on the bottom floor. Bedrooms, a television room and a study are housed on the intermediate floors.

In order to create a sense of connectedness between the five split floors a void was punched through the floor plates. This provides views, light and acts as a reference point on each floor.

Building fabric was updated to make the house more energy efficient and robust. The external felted finish of the original roof was removed and a crisp black-zinc roof added as a durable and contemporary replacement. The internal balsa wood, a prominent feature of the home's original design, was retained and carefully refurbished.

Despite the relatively superficial nature of the works carried out, this new design succeeded in bringing an ageing house into the 21st century.

Upper floor plan

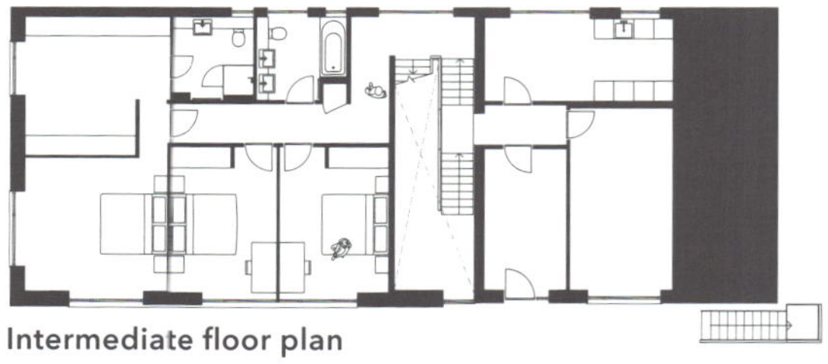

Intermediate floor plan

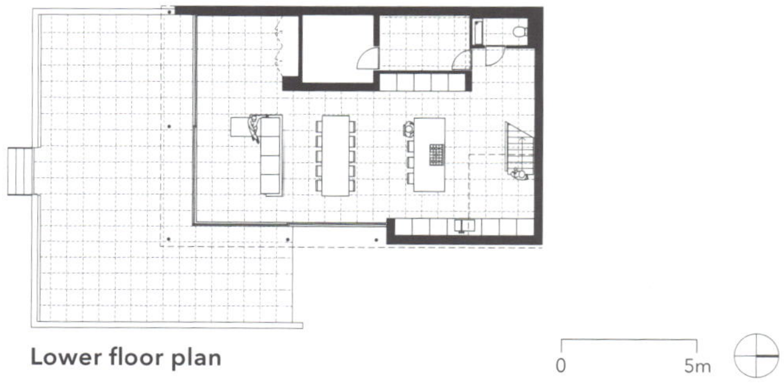

Lower floor plan

PROJECT SPECIFICATIONS

Location: Winchester, Hampshire, England

Area: 460 m^2 (4951 ft^2)

Completed: 2014

Photography: Martin Gardner (pages 93, 94, 95, 96); Mike French (page 97)

The garden is an integral part of the overall ground-floor plan because it mirrors and interlocks with the house plan. By introverting the external garden area into the design of the house, the site area is maximised without any impact on the adjoining dwellings. This concept allows the ground floor to be as open as possible, taking advantage of the site's southwest orientation. The laneway façade is designed as a defensive or boundary wall, pierced only by small openings with timber louvre screens. On the garden side, in sharp contrast, full-height glazing allows maximum penetration of light deep into the plan from the south and west façades.

The first-floor level has been treated similarly to the ground floor, with all windows focused around a planted sedum roof. This south-facing roof garden and full-height glazing allows light to penetrate deep into the bedrooms without the possibility of direct or indirect overlooking from adjoining properties. The Iroko louvres at the ground floor extend up to the first-floor level to form a privacy screen.

The openness and transparency of the south and west façades at the ground-floor level juxtapose sharply with the closed treatment of the east and north façades, which have been left as solid brick planes to ensure no overlooking of adjoining gardens. The first-floor brick-clad box accentuates the solidity of these inward looking sculptural volumes. The uncompromising outward façade projects a determination to ensure the privacy of those inside and of those in surrounding houses.

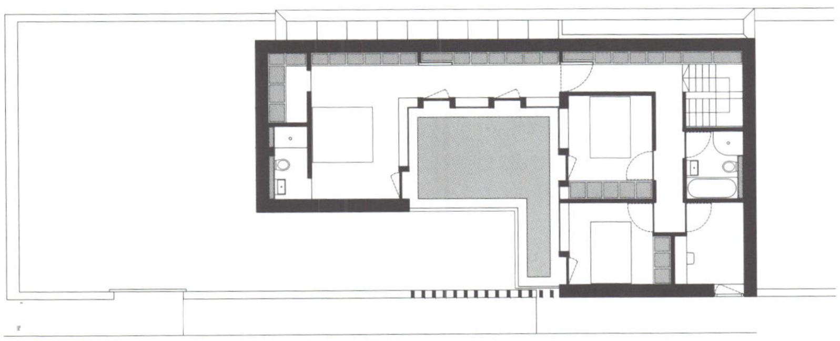

First-floor plan

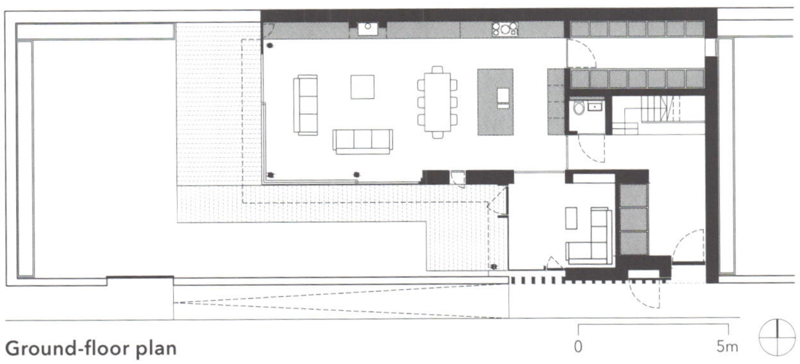

Ground-floor plan

PROJECT SPECIFICATIONS

Location: Clontarf, Dublin, Ireland
Area: 180 m^2 (1938 ft^2)
Completed: 2015
Photography: Alice Clancy

Jestico + Whiles

HOUSE 19

This project is a carbon-neutral, energy efficient home that fuses traditional forms and local materials in an elegant, modern way to make full use of the natural aspect and orientation of its site.

An entrance gallery leads to the main body of the house, with bedrooms on the upper level and large picture windows framing considered views. The house modulates daylight internally to dramatic effect, resulting in a tranquil atmosphere that changes throughout the seasons. Kitchen, dining and living spaces combine to create a family hub with visual and physical connections to the south-facing garden. A single-storey studio has the flexibility of being used as a garden room, office or ground floor bedroom.

Practical and deliverable sustainability features form the bedrock of the design. The home features a ground source heat pump, earth tube ventilation, photovoltaic panels and rainwater harvesting. A double-height space at the heart of the plan works at an architectural level uniting the two floors, but is also a passive stack, allowing high-level vents that open during summer to create natural cooling.

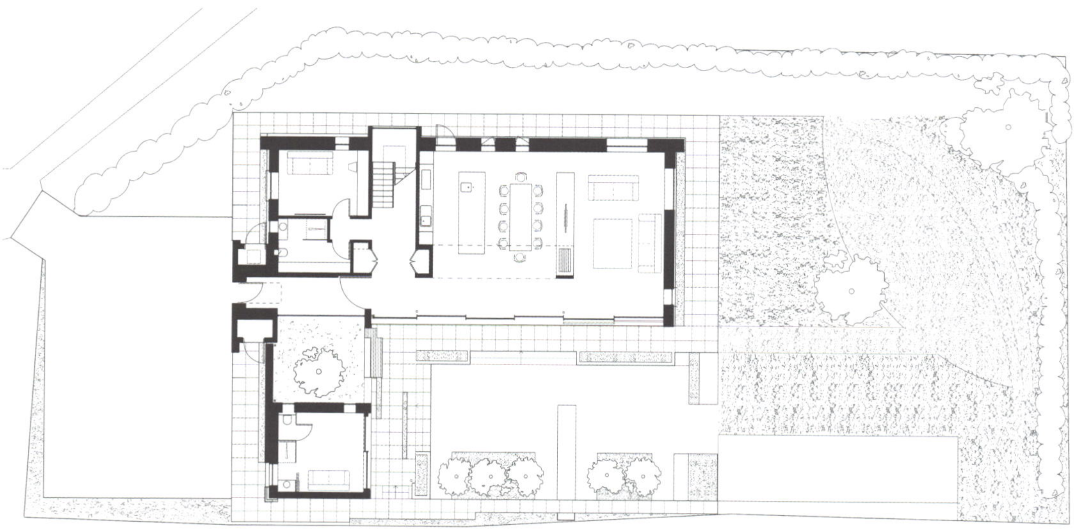

Ground-floor plan

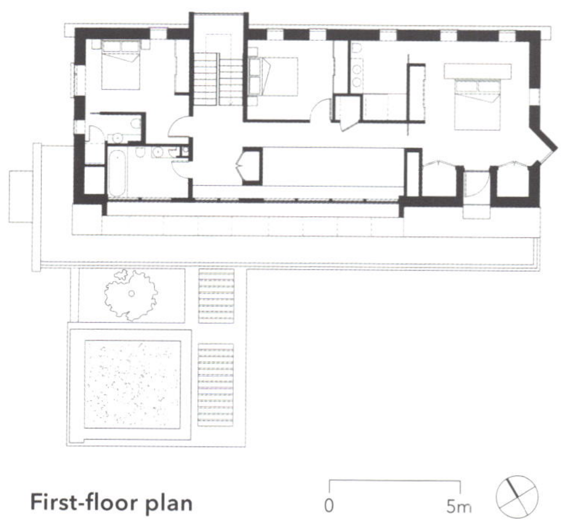

First-floor plan

Materials are locally sourced and firmly rooted in the history of the area. Black-stained cedar cladding echoes agricultural barn buildings; the local church inspires the snapped-and-knapped luminescent flint; and Corten steel accents have been chosen to reflect rusty deposits found on the flint.

Expressing the two storeys on the northeast elevation and reducing the height on the southern elevation to a single storey by means of an eccentrically pitched roof, means that the impact on the adjoining property is minimised. This, together with the materiality of the house means it adopts a commanding yet respectful presence in the context of its neighbourhood.

PROJECT SPECIFICATIONS

Location: Old Amersham, Buckinghamshire, England

Area: 246 m^2 (2648 ft^2)

Completed: 2016

Photography: Grant Smith

This house was conceived as a simple two-storey villa placed in the centre of a flat rectangular site surrounded by mature trees. The ground-floor spaces are defined by a series of interconnecting white-painted brick walls, with full-height glazing between. The plan of the house and arrangement of these walls divides the garden into four quadrants, each with a different theme.

Open-plan kitchen and dining spaces are at ground level and arranged around a top-lit, double-height stairwell, which also acts as a gallery space. The gallery bleeds into adjoining spaces with paintings carefully positioned in each. These spaces have strong connections to formal and informal garden areas. The upper level, a timber-clad volume with screened windows and carved out balconies, contains the family's private quarters and includes bathrooms lit only from above.

shedkm

HOUSE FOR AN ART LOVER

Externally, the home is clearly articulated with a simple palette of materials. Whitewashed brick, Iroko cladding and timber-framed glazing bring scale and a more domestic feel to the large volumes. Careful arrangement of formal and informal planting bed the house into its setting.

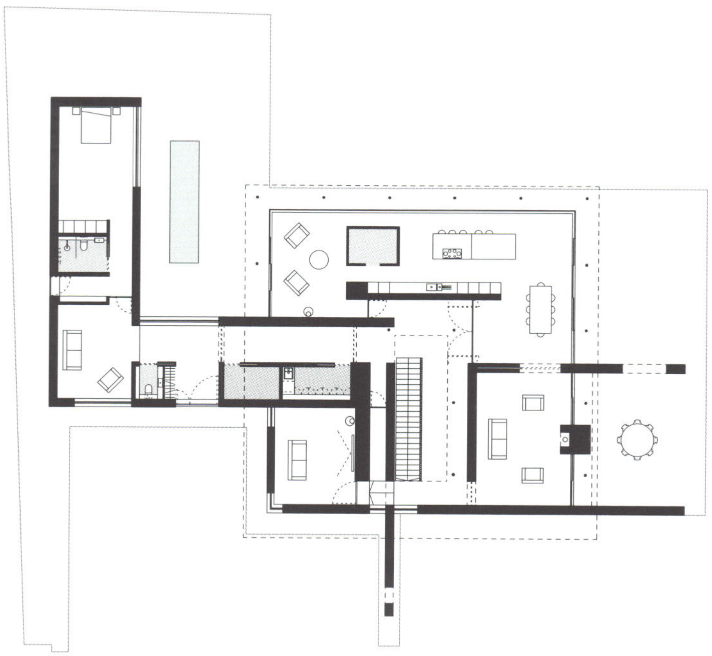
Ground-floor plan

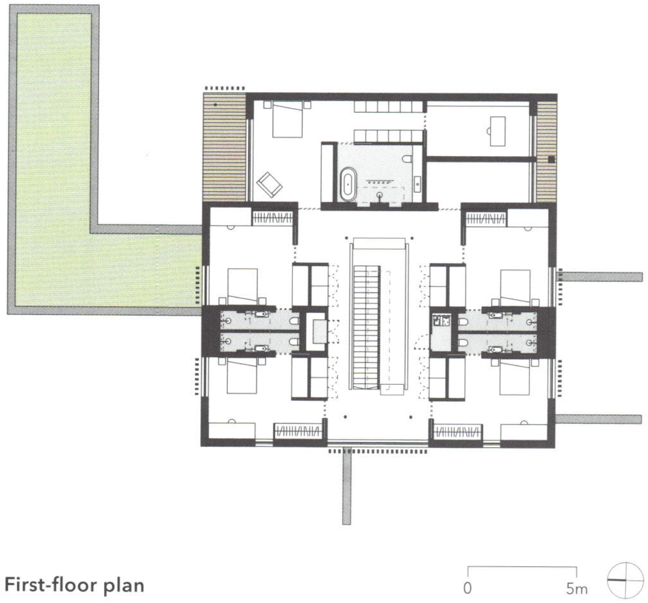
First-floor plan
0
5m

PROJECT SPECIFICATIONS

Location: Merseyside, England
Area: 650 m^2 (6997 ft^2)
Completed: 2014
Photography: Jack Hobhouse

After the demolition of an original extension, this home required an intervention that would honour the original building whilst simultaneously allowing the new project to have its own identity.

The original extension had no distinct historical or architectural value and was structurally unsound. The architects chose to incorporate the home's sloping roof – a typical terrace house feature – into the new face of the rear garden, preserving its charm and a sense of memory. The new envelope's structures have been internally exposed wherever practically possible, with the intent of registering future stories of the house.

Tsuruta Architects

HOUSE OF TRACE

The hand marks of bare plaster finish left exposed in the bedrooms are now recorded on the internal faces of the building's fabric. The slow patination of bespoke copper and brass fittings reflect a passage of time as they change from their original colour. In response to the home's increased depth, a two-storey lightwell was added between the new and original part of the building, bringing daylight to interior rooms. The lightwell serves as a focal point in the home, connecting the family between floors (open kitchen, dining level and bedrooms).

On the upper floor, the master bedroom and children's room each has an internal window facing the lightwell. This gives the parents and children a sense of one another's presence whilst also allowing for privacy when desired.

The entire building and its new components were three dimensionally modelled. Some components, including the main stair and furniture were further broken down and processed with CNC (Computer Numerical Control). They were then brought to the site as flat-pack packages, which significantly cut project cost and time. A record of the CNC flat-pack process was deliberately left visible on the faces of each piece, retaining memories of assembly within the home long after project completion. Materials used include: facing bricks, exposed steel, white cement concrete, aluminium, timber, composite frame windows, pine-board panels, birch plywood, melamine plywood, coloured MDF (solid), glazed subway tiles, and copper pipes with brass garden taps. The project reveals memories of place and registers future stories, allowing the past and present to coexist in a brand new home.

PROJECT SPECIFICATIONS

Location: London, England
Area: 110 m^2 (1184 ft^2)
Completed: 2015
Photography: Tim Crocker

Adam Knibb Architects

HURDLE HOUSE

Adam Knibb Architects were approached to put together a contemporary extension for a Grade II–listed house in Alresford. Hurdle House has a long history within the village, having been part of the original sheep fairs back in 1792. The clients wanted a contemporary addition that would maintain respect for the original barn.

The scheme was approached with an aim to set works into the surrounding nature, provide natural light, harness the fantastic views, and provide a social heart to the house. Working with the Winchester conservation department, it was agreed that the rear bay window could be removed to provide a linking element to the extension. A frameless glass link was envisaged, touching the existing building lightly and connecting the old to the new. The extension comprises a large open-plan kitchen, dining area, casual seating with utility and water closet, and attached study.

A major aim of the project was to increase excitement upon entering the property. The new main entrance directly introduces this proposal, showing off beautiful views of the garden. Vertical timber cladding provides a contemporary contrast to the existing building and mimics the surrounding trees. With large glass apertures, the property's natural surrounds blur boundaries of the extension, making the home a prime example of contemporary architecture at harmony with the natural landscape.

Theatre, drama and illusion are central to the architecture of Infinity House.

It is an exciting sequence of contrasting spaces, which interconnect in a variety of ways to create a unique spatial experience. This design led, rejuvenation project substantially extends an 18th-century Georgian townhouse after removing a poor quality industrial workshop that covered the original garden.

Spaced Out Ltd

INFINITY HOUSE

The sanctuary and classic section of the townhouse has been seamlessly linked vertically and horizontally to new spaces. Soft reflections and floating details deliver transitions between the old, new and nature. The structured planting of sky gardens, visible from all main spaces, invites nature into the home.

The home's glazing is impressive, with Hepco Motion applying its automated sliding technology to create the UK's widest vertical motorised sash window. Glazing has also been used in other areas of the house, enabling privacy or interconnectedness at the touch of a button. The home boasts a variety of dramatic and multi-directional views, connecting features such as the swimming pool to the sky.

Smart controls and recyclable energy have been implemented throughout the home. This enables efficient and easy-to-run spaces whilst seamlessly combining traditional architectural craft-based techniques with digital technology. Privacy, as an example, is managed with carefully selected planting and traditional shutters alongside interactive glass interlayers.

There are numerous special moments, great spaces and details that create the undeniable theatre of this unique London townhouse.

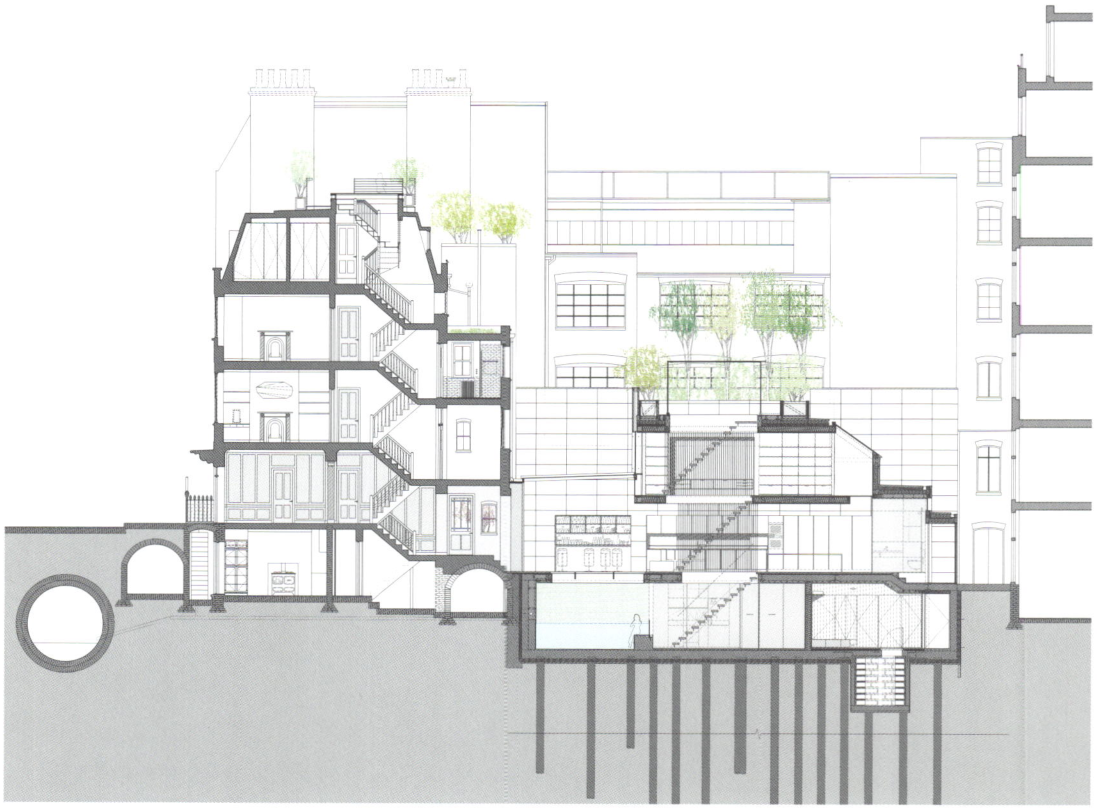

Long section

PROJECT SPECIFICATIONS

Location: London, England
Area: 500 m² (5382 ft²)
Completed: 2016
Photography: www.joshphoto.com

This project radically transforms a 1950s house into a unique and highly efficient home suitable for a young family. The client's brief sought to create a low energy home that was architectural yet restrained. New insulation and bricks, which envelope the building, improve the home's thermal performance and give it a fresh identity.

Careful and considered brick detailing reflects the client's fastidious attention to detail and helps to control façade proportions.

Chiles Evans + Care Architects

KNOWLE HOUSE

From the street, the house is deliberately restrained: a simple two-storey mass of brickwork retaining many of the window openings of the original house, capped by a slate-clad roof. A low-sweeping, timber canopy projects from the front of the house, suggesting that the external form belies the internal experience.

109

The house is entered from street level via a low, timber-lined entrance. This gives way to a triple-height stairwell, which links all of levels of the house. At the first-floor level, ceilings follow the new roofline, creating a dynamic conclusion to the stairwell. The panoramic window of the lounge space on the upper-ground level reveals the dramatic topography hidden from the street. The deep timber reveal creates a space to sit and look over the garden below as well as towards the white peak beyond.

The lower-ground floor forms an enfilade of rooms designed to allow for different activities to take place in adjacent spaces and to bring the family together.

Deeply recessed, glazed elements frame views across the wide terrace and over the trees at the foot of the garden. A herb garden and raised lawn complement the terraced area and further blur visual edges with the wider landscape. Generous brick-lined steps lead to the informal garden below.

PROJECT SPECIFICATIONS

Location: Yorkshire, England
Area: 1890 m^2 (20,344 ft^2)
Completed: 2016
Photography: Jeremy Phillips

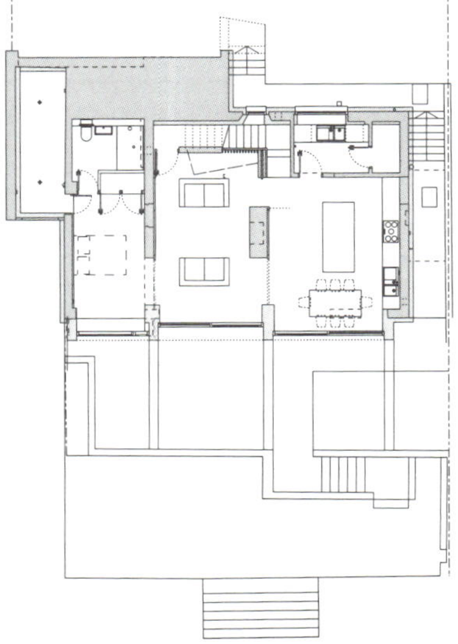

Lower floor plan

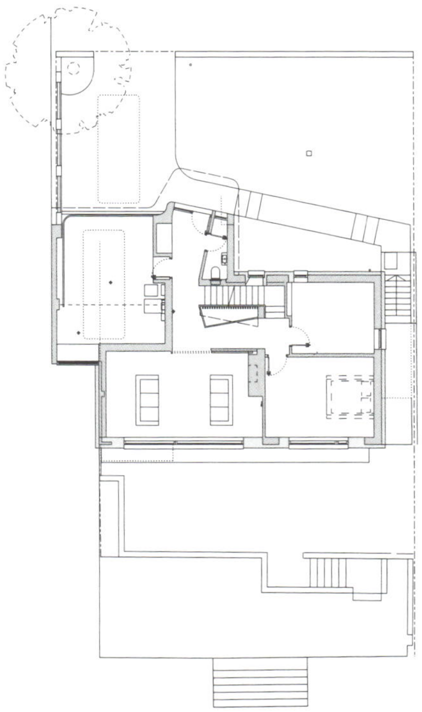

Ground-floor plan

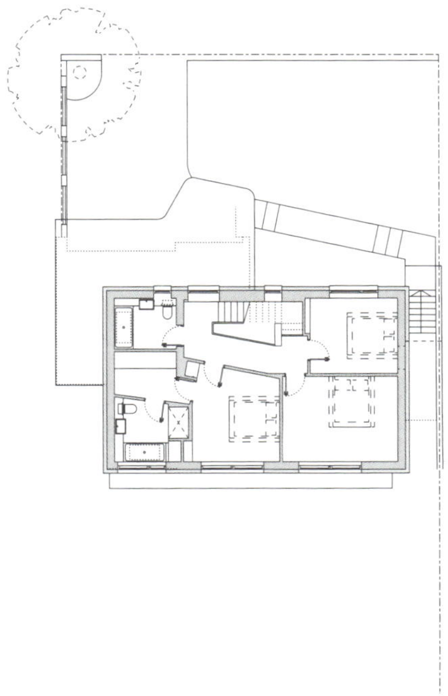

First-floor plan

Hudson Architects

LE PETIT FORT

This home sits on the shoreline of St Ouen's Bay and occupies the site of an earlier, now demolished, farmstead. The original building was constructed in the early 20th century and enclosed within thick granite walls, which have been retained and restored. The house was conceived to complete the 'fort' concept by building the missing fourth wall of the enclosure and creating a central element to represent a 'keep'.

The three-storey entrance block, like the perimeter walls, was constructed from Jersey granite and reclaimed from the earlier building. A pair of two-storey wings radiates from this block, dividing the walled enclosure into an entrance forecourt and sheltered garden, and enclosing a landscaped pool terrace. The two wings use a contrasting palette of contemporary materials: polished micro-cement render down to the ground floor sits below an oversailing and highly textured first floor of Corten and Iroko panelling. The first floor shelters the entrance and ground floor terraces, whilst the deep eaves shade a first-floor balcony and enhance the building's distinctive silhouette.

The composition offers a lively series of contrasting profiles from different viewpoints. From the entrance the fort-like character dominates, picking up references to nearby Napoleonic Martello towers and Second World War fortifications. Small windows set into the Corten panelling give the house a robust and intriguing presence. From the beach, the house appears as a low-set watchtower, with the keep and first floor peering over the top of the granite walls. From the pool terrace, the building assumes a more welcoming and transparent character.

PROJECT SPECIFICATIONS

Location: St Ouen's Bay, Jersey, Channel Islands
Area: 472 m^2 (5081 ft^2)
Completed: 2015
Photography: Joakim Boren (pages 141, 142-3); Edmund Summer (pages 144, 145)

Inside, the main living area occupies the first floor of the sea-facing wing, with impressive views across the bay through full-height windows, which lead onto a balcony and terrace. The open-plan space is broken up by level changes: low dividing walls and a feature fireplace facing two sitting areas. The master-bedroom suite in the opposite wing is linked by a large landing, which provides additional relaxation space. The ground floor contains family bedrooms, a media room, sauna, laundry, and plant room. The main floors are linked by a stunning spiral staircase, which is lit from above by a conical lantern rising through the 'keep'. A smaller yet similarly crafted concrete spiral staircase leads to a study and guest-bedroom suite at the top of the house.

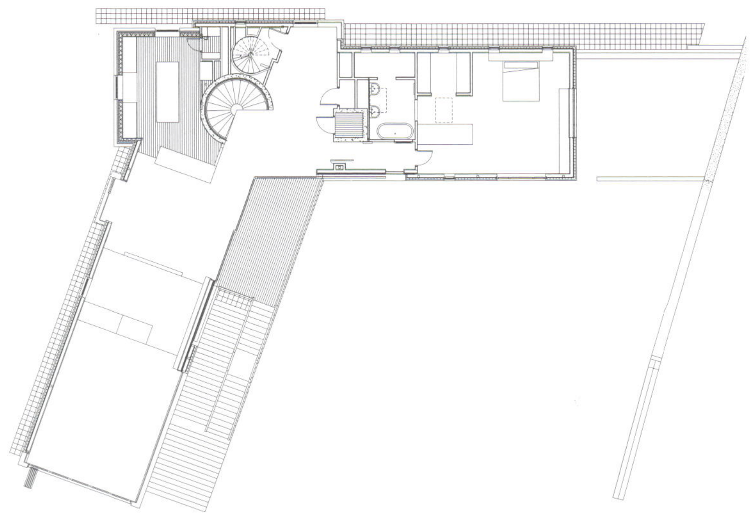

First-floor plan

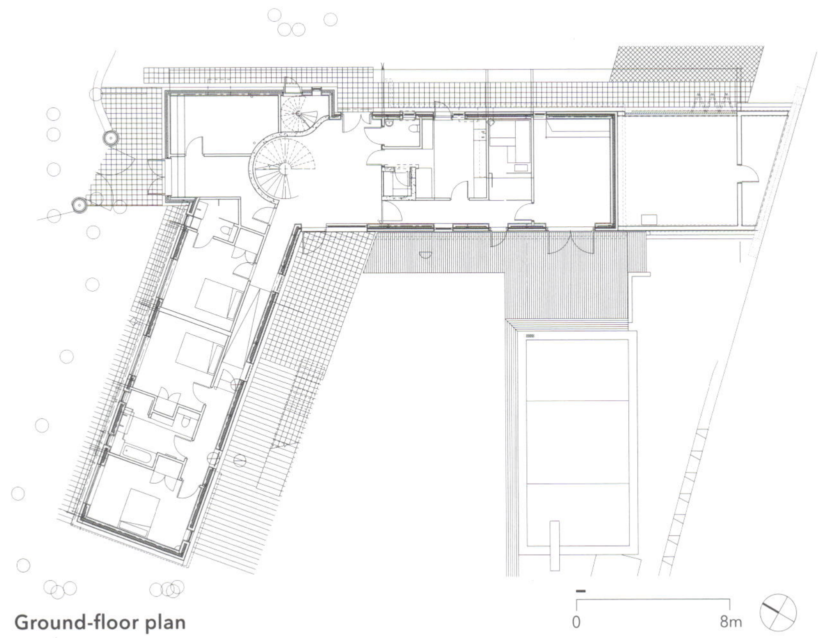

Ground-floor plan

Located in the heart of Kew conservation, this typical detached property was built to mimic the traditional Edwardian houses next door. The home lacked the detail and craftsmanship expected of homes within historical vicinities. Its dormers were set too high, denying garden views; the main staircase opposite the entrance hall appeared dark; and several level changes within the home gave a dated impression.

3S Architects and Designers

LION GATE GARDENS

The architects worked with the owners to fundamentally improve the home's interior flow. A large rear extension was added to the home. This allowed for a spacious living area with a kitchen at the upper floor leading down into a dining area.

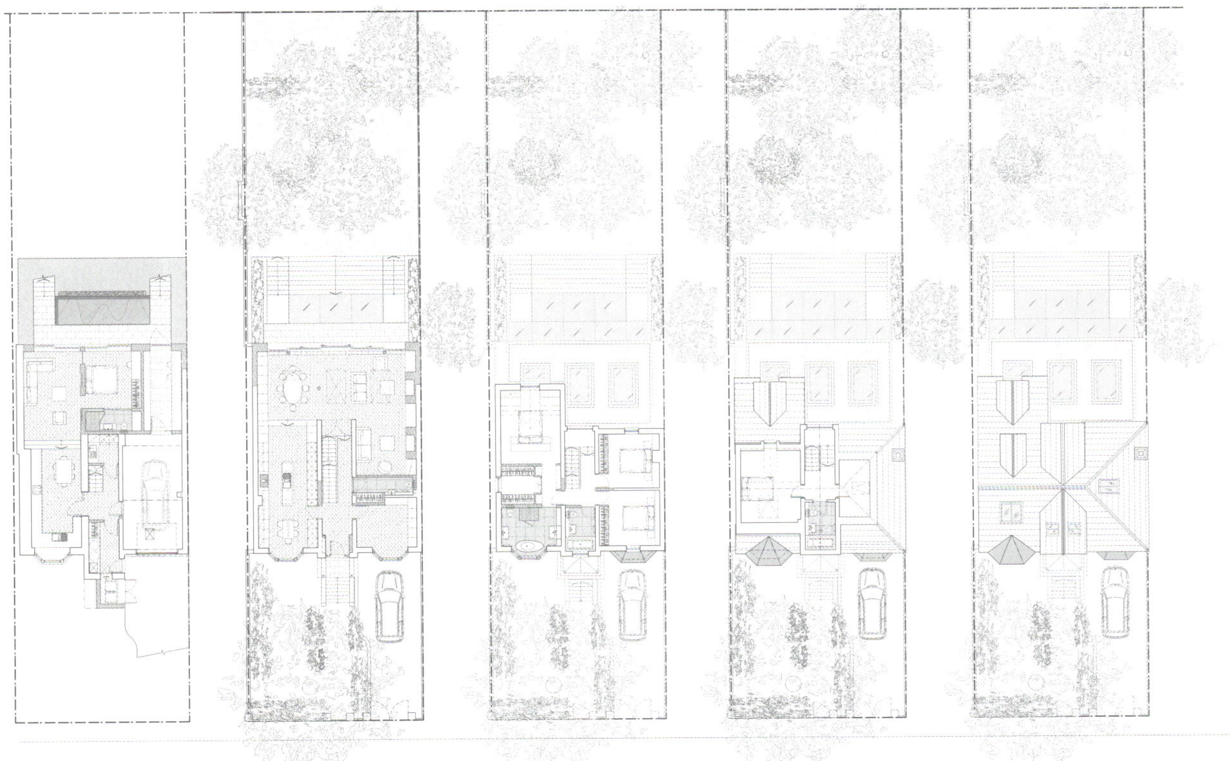

Basement floor plan Ground-floor plan First-floor plan Second-floor plan Roof floor plan 0 8m

The low ceilings of the existing basement were replaced with higher ceilings and a separate guest bedroom with moving walls. This space can also be used as a study/lounge, second kitchen or storage utility.

The upper bedrooms have been practically designed, with ample storage and spacious bathrooms. These spaces connect to a new stairway, which winds along an all-glass skin down to the basement. A clever mix of styles – New York loft meets Philip Stark – gives the home a feeling of city life.

PROJECT SPECIFICATIONS

Location: London, England
Area: 77 m^2 (829 ft^2)
Completed: 2015
Photography: Alistair Nicholls

SAM Architects

MAP HOUSE

Although the initial site for this home was particularly small – 7 metres by 7 metres (23 feet by 23 feet) – the architects sought to devise a beautiful design that would work within the unique London location. The aim was to create a home that would fit coherently within area's historic urban fabric, whilst being unashamedly modern and adhering to the owners' lifestyles.

The external fabric is a traditional cavity wall construction made of 150-year-old reclaimed dark bricks and special order black mortar. The bricks are laid with wide flush joints to create a continuous surface emphasising the joint instead of the brick. Minimal windows, gunmetal grey in colour, blend in with the tones of the walls and reinforce the perception of a simple and unitary aboveground mass.

First-floor plan

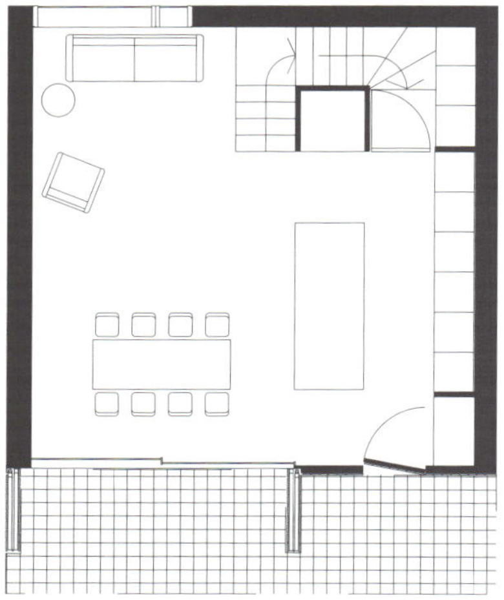

Ground-floor plan

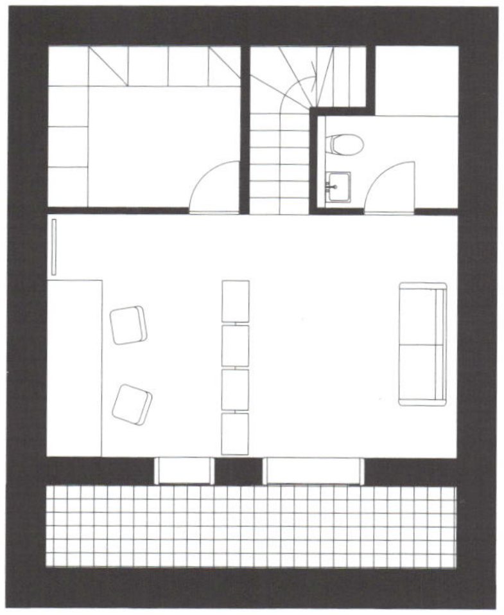

Basement floor plan

On the mews side, the ground floor has been clad in charred-larch slats, which counterpoint the solidity of the brick volume with a lightly articulated vertical texture. A large part of this façade is an automated bi-folding gate, which opens to reveal a 3-metre by 4-metre (10-foot by 13-foot) glass wall, allowing the living space to be at one with the outdoors on warm summer days. From the inside, the open gates frame a view to the gardens and provide a sense of privacy from passers-by.

PROJECT SPECIFICATIONS

Location: London, England
Area: 49 m² (527 ft²)
Completed: 2015
Photography: Edmund Sumner

An open-plan kitchen and dining area, with an open stair leading to the first floor welcome entry into the home. This stair is topped with a large roof light, which brightens the ground floor. On the first floor there are two bedrooms and a generous bathroom. From the kitchen area, the lower-ground level can be accessed via the stair through a hidden door. The basement is provided light by a 1.5-metre-wide (5-foot-wide) light well with a galvanised grill, which sits at the front of the house. This area also includes a guest room, shower room, utility room, and study.

Materials used include oak, concrete, white plaster, charred timber, and bricks. Charred timber and bricks were the only materials used externally. The bespoke kitchen was designed as a workshop with very simple and hardwearing materials, such as plywood and linoleum.

This bespoke home replaces a small existing house, which had become neglected and incompatible with contemporary family life. The design approach was to derive a modern aesthetic from local vernacular architecture whilst maintaining a fundamental commitment to issues of sustainability.

The external finishes have been horizontally arranged with black timber at the first floor stacked onto a plinth of knapped flint. These materials are present in vernacular buildings nearby. The first floor is articulated as a series of boxes, which shift back and forth, providing the ground floor with roof lights and solar shading.

Cassion Castle Architects

OAK LANE HOUSE

Approached via a northern courtyard, the building initially appears as somewhat impenetrable and monolithic, but upon entering the interior reveals itself to be surprisingly light and open with a strong sense of transparency. Interior spaces were designed as a blank canvas so that the client – a keen interior designer – could make her mark over time. Polished concrete, oak parquet, natural stone, and a simple decorative palette give the house a timeless and elegant identity.

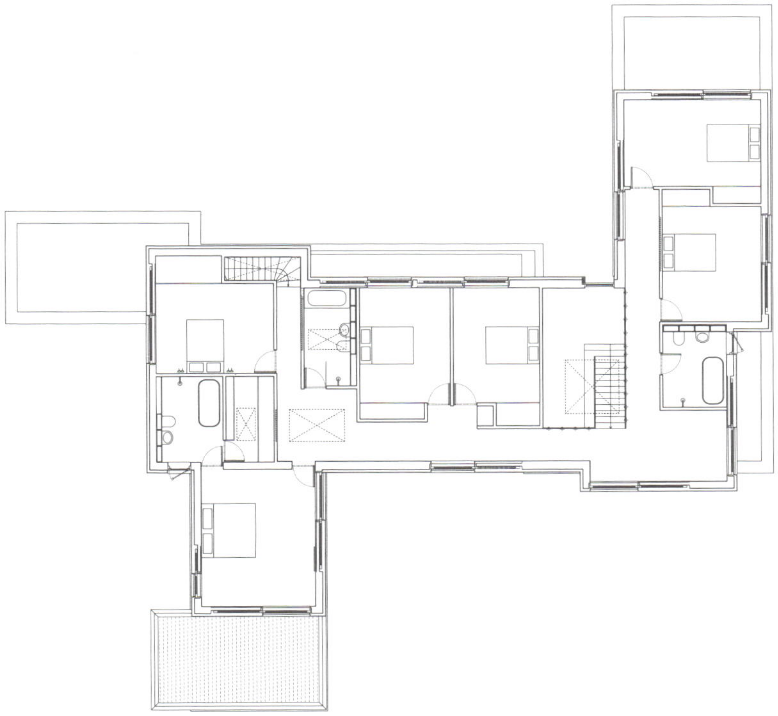

First-floor plan

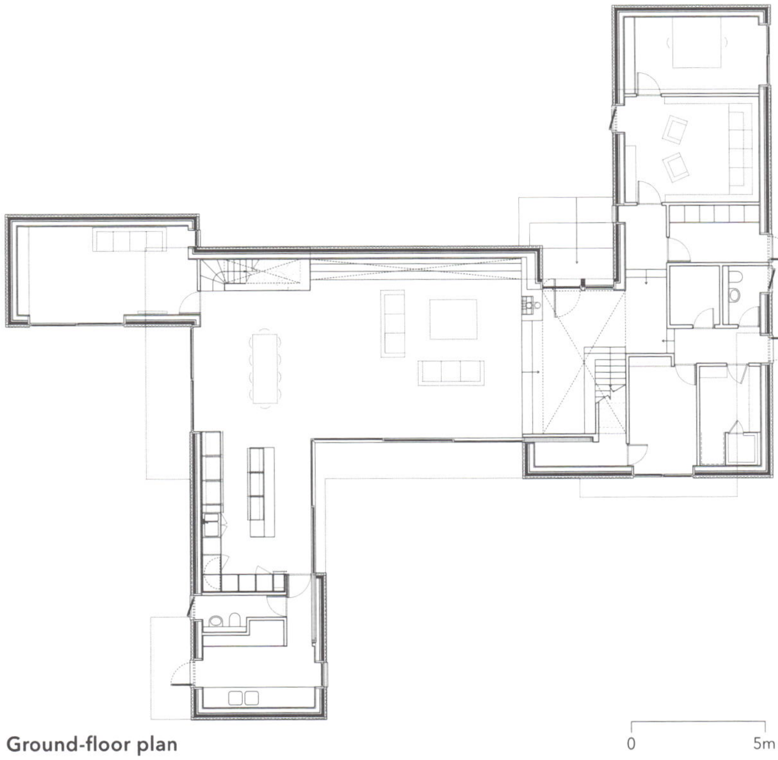

Ground-floor plan

Steel frame construction enabled a fast build and permitted the building's many cantilevers. A storey-height truss incorporated into the wall at first-floor level enabled the living room's wide, clear spans.

Inspired by local farm buildings, the ground floor has been separated into wings, which define external spaces around the home. These intermediary spaces create a relationship between the building and landscape: a welcoming north-facing entrance courtyard, a contemplative orchard, a large south-facing open garden, and a smaller west-facing children's garden. A double-height entrance hall leads to a generous central wing, which is broken into clearly defined zones for cooking, dining and relaxing. Large sliding doors disappear into cavity walls to provide a seamless transition from the interior through to the terrace and into the garden. The ground floor also contains a library, study, gym, playroom, utility, and boot room. Six bedrooms and bathrooms are accommodated within the timber blocks upstairs.

C

The home was designed to be highly sustainable. The first floor overhangs the ground floor and is set back on the north elevation. This creates a north-facing roof light and prevents overheating in summer. Rubble from the existing building was recycled and used for the new house. Other energy saving measures include photovoltaic panels, low-energy fixtures, a woodchip burning stove, and a biomass boiler powered by a sewage processing bio-digester.

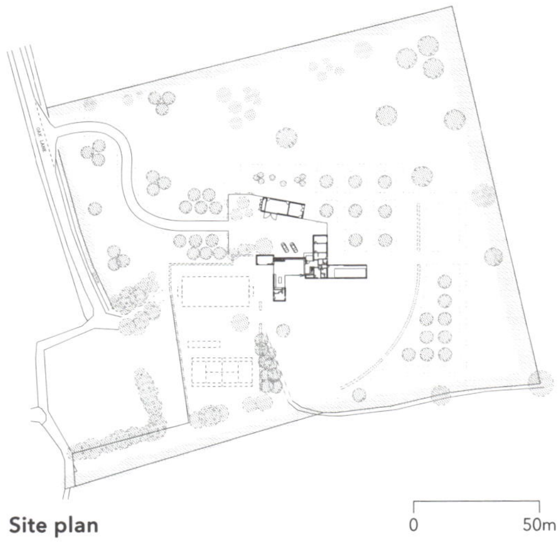

Site plan

PROJECT SPECIFICATIONS

Location: Suffolk, England

Area: 450 m² (4844 ft²)

Completed: 2015

Photography: Kilian O'Sullivan

Broadstone Architects

OAKLANDS

A primary characteristic of these particular mid-20th century houses is the large rear façade chimney. Given the height and presence of this home's chimney stack and its balance with the neighbouring equivalent, the architects decided to make it a focal point in the roof design, off which all extending roof pitches would generate.

In order to utilise the western aspect along the boundary of the sizeable rear garden, an extension stretches into the garden. This maintains light, ventilation and views to and from the original rear façade via a courtyard. Conscious of the neighbour's daylight aspect and long extending building, the architects formed the roof shape with low pitches, which spring from the main existing chimney stack. These low-rising angles are brought further into the extension to direct light; similar to how the roof rises to capture clerestory light.

The single-storey extension wraps around a new courtyard, allowing south and west light into the centre of the plan, whilst catching glimpses of the long landscaped garden. An external fireplace and stone gully for a rainwater spout add aspect to the courtyard, which is accessed from the kitchen and dining areas. A living room terminates the extension and opens into the garden, availing evening light with south-facing clerestory windows above the boundary wall. The bevelled canopy and edge wall enclose and hide utility access to the garden.

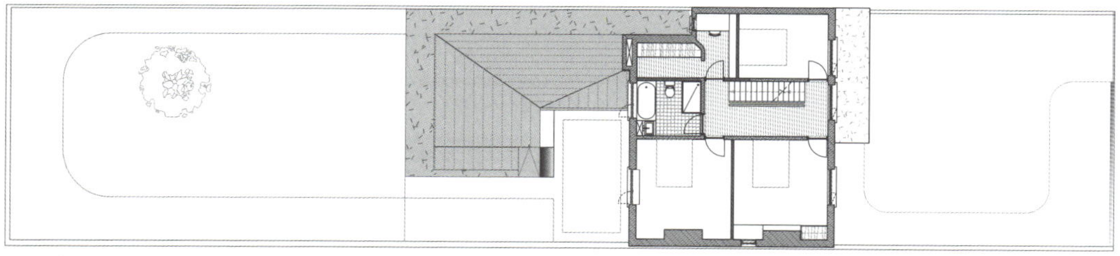

First-floor plan

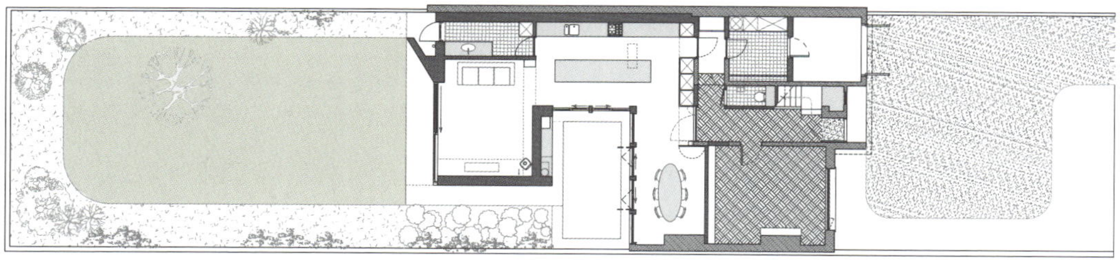

Ground-floor plan

The kitchen is central and acts as a hub from which all areas can be be accessed. A full refurbishment of the main house provides a new staircase with change of direction. This allows daylight into the hall and provides access to the attic. Materials chosen include post-finished concrete and limewashed birch plywood, which complement the original industrial-style steel windows.

PROJECT SPECIFICATIONS

Location: Dublin, Ireland

Area: 204 m^2 (2196 ft^2)

Completed: 2016

Photography: Aisling McCoy

The Old Water Tower is a passively certified four-bedroom family home on the edge of Chieveley in West Berkshire.

The project was conceived as a modern interpretation of the timber-framed barns within the area, those that when seen at a distance appear as simple, traditional and agricultural buildings. On closer inspection, The Old Water Tower reveals itself as a crisply designed, carefully made contemporary interpretation of the historic buildings it draws inspiration from.

Gresford Architects

THE OLD WATER TOWER

The architects aimed to create a home that would eschew austere interpretations of eco-friendly living, whilst remaining on the cutting edge of sustainable design. The result is a home that is extremely easy to live yet costs virtually nothing to run. Space on the roof for photovoltaic and solar thermal panels provides the option of total self-reliance.

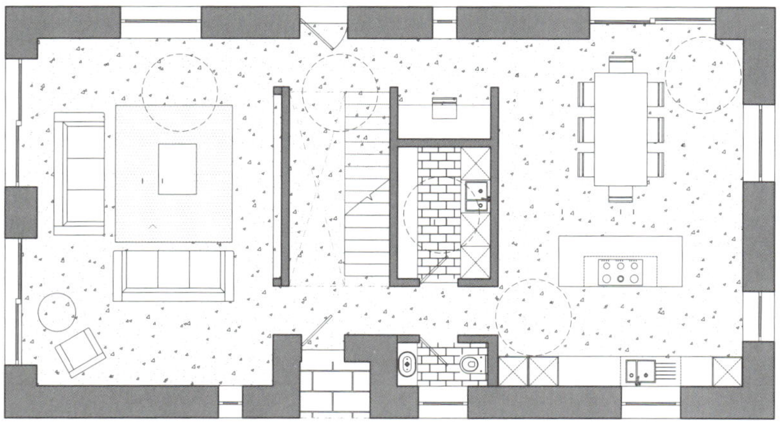

Ground-floor plan

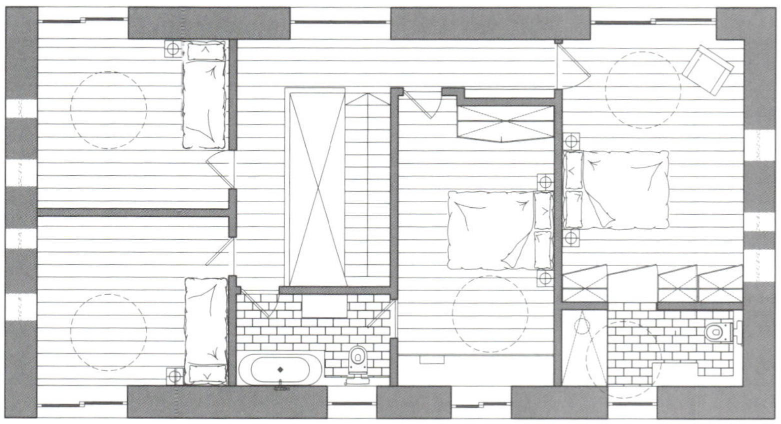

First-floor plan

PROJECT SPECIFICATIONS

Location: Chieveley, West Berkshire, England
Area: 173 m^2 (1862 ft^2)
Completed: 2015
Photography: Quintin Lake

Another critical aspect involved in passive house construction is the internal level of comfort a home provides year round. This was achieved by installing a mechanical ventilation and heat recovery unit, which provides constant background ventilation by removing stale air and drawing in fresh air. This creates a fresh and ventilated feeling within the home, whilst maintaining warmth.

The house has openable triple-glazed windows and large triple-glazed sliding doors. To reduce the risk of overheating, external blinds on the east, south, and west elevation automatically deploy when the home's internal temperature reaches 21°C (69.8°F).

McCullough Mulvin Architects

ONE UP TWO DOWN

One Up Two Down is an urban courtyard house in central Dublin built on a very tight budget. The site was carved out of an existing plot along the now in-filled Royal Canal.

The home's scheme fills the rectangular site and maximises open space. Loft-like living space on the upper floor allows for privacy, light and views. Below are bedrooms and a studio, which sit beyond the central courtyard. Nature is at the heart of the house. A walled and stepped garden planted with vegetables, grasses and wild flowers is located at the front of the home. A planted central courtyard, roof terrace and upper-roof sky garden provide additional green spaces for the owners to enjoy.

At the home's entrance, a light-filled staircase leads to the main living space and stretches between the island kitchen and seating area, directing views out toward the studio terrace.

Bricks from the original ruined house were salvaged and re-used to anchor the front façade. A screen of wooden Iroko ribs over a glass and timber elevation, giving the front of the home a striking identity. The ribs continue along the upper level of the central courtyard and have been angled to bring in sunlight and screen views. Internally, finishes are austere and simple – polished concrete floors, white-painted exposed rafters, and Iroko windows and doors.

PROJECT SPECIFICATIONS

Location: Dublin, Ireland
Area: 170 m^2 (1830 ft^2)
Completed: 2016
Photography: Courtesy of the architect

The new rear wing on the ground floor encloses on the western boundary to form a courtyard intermediary between the original property and the new extended living area. An existing building footprint and a mature mountain ash tree generated the form of this zinc-clad wing. The extension leans away from the tree's canopy, pitching in height towards the house to create a vaulted ceiling over the new dining and living area, and lowering towards the courtyard to preserve sunlight access to the existing ground-floor rooms and garden outlook from the first-floor bedroom window. Openings in the existing external wall were maintained and provide access points to the new extension.

The original external fabric of the building was preserved and integrated into the extension. What were side windows looking directly to a boundary fence are now portals that allow circulation between the kitchen and new living area. Wide glass sliding doors frame new view lines established to the full length of the property. Whilst sequence has been preserved, these spaces are now interlinked by views to the courtyard, living wing and garden beyond, improving the daylight and vista quality of the interior without augmenting its spatial typology.

PROJECT SPECIFICATIONS

Location: North London, England
Area: 181 m² (1948 ft²)
Completed: 2015
Photography: David Butler

Inside the home, the soft grey hues and timber features of the original rooms contrast with the white walls and black-framed metal windows of the new additions. Externally, the graphite-zinc cladding defines new elements of the existing slate and brick. The subtleties of these differences are a result of meaningful interventions, which serve to define the property's history whilst giving it a unified elegance.

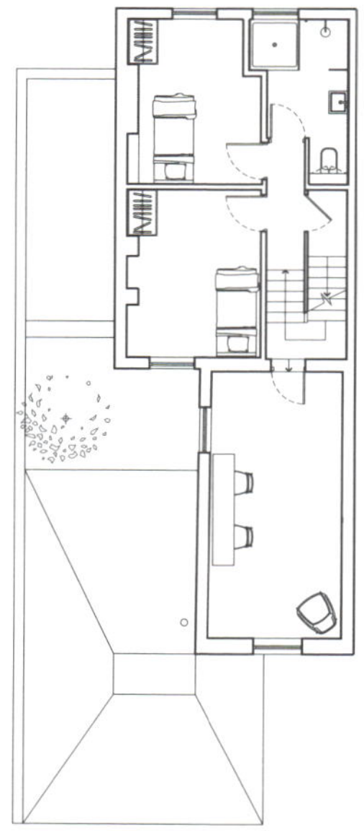

First-floor plan

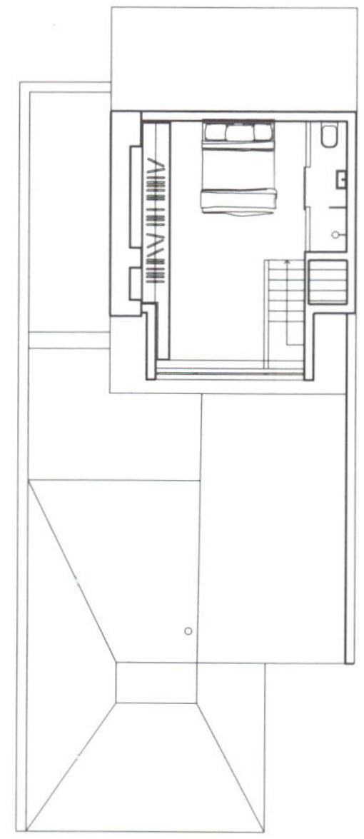

Second-floor plan

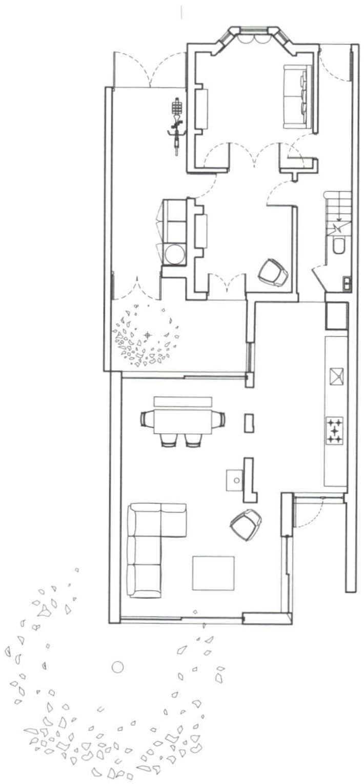

Ground-floor plan

Pennycroft is a five-bedroom family home that replaces an outdated 1930s house on a semi-rural plot. To comply with the area's strict planning policy the design is a contemporary interpretation of the local Arts and Crafts architecture. It has been positioned to occupy the front of the plot and align with adjacent properties.

Napier Clarke Architects

PENNYCROFT

The concept is simple – a brick base, punctured with a series of apertures supports clerestory windows with timber detailing above. Mirrored on both sides of the home, glass gables rise to an apex set within a high-pitched roof. Locally sourced, handmade brick with lime mortar softens the contemporary appearance.

The new build comprises two separate structural elements: a large two-storey building and a vaulted single-storey living space. These are linked via a glass walkway, which allows the volumes to read separately whilst physically joining to create an L-shaped footprint orientated to frame the rear garden. Two perpendicular axes inform the internal layout of the building and create a strong visual and physical connection from one end of the home to the other. From these axes, a sequence of single-volume spaces tuck behind partitioning walls, creating a balance between open and enclosed space.

The main entrance reveals a double-height hallway with a high timber-clad vaulted ceiling. Upstairs, a gallery landing bridges this space and physically separates family bedrooms from the guest suite, providing each side with privacy. Large expanses of glazing throughout the home flood spaces with an abundance of natural light.

Adopting a sustainable approach was a key aspect of the home's design. The crushed aggregate from the existing house was used as a sub base for the new project. To resolve a two-meter slope on site, the building has been excavated into the ground to minimise visual disturbance to adjacent properties. Low U-values have been achieved through optimum provision of insulation on external walls, therefore reducing the need for artificial heating. High G-value, double-glazing works in combination with the deep timber reveals on the upper storey, providing subtle solar shading to the south-facing façade and allowing for large expanses of glass.

Locally sourced Bovingdon red brick with lime mortar wraps around the entirety of the lower floor and all timber is FSC-certified Douglas fir.

This project successfully integrates into its sensitive surroundings and provides the client with a distinctive new home, one that meets the requirements of modern living.

PROJECT SPECIFICATIONS

Location: Great Missenden, Buckinghamshire, England
Area: 430 m² (4628 ft²)
Completed: 2016
Photography: Joakim Borén

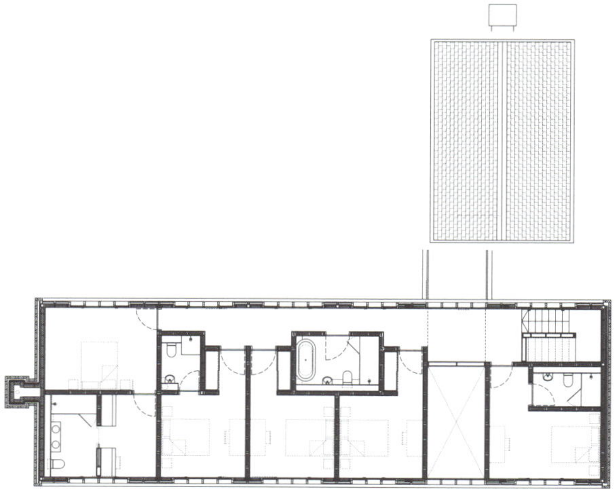

First-floor plan

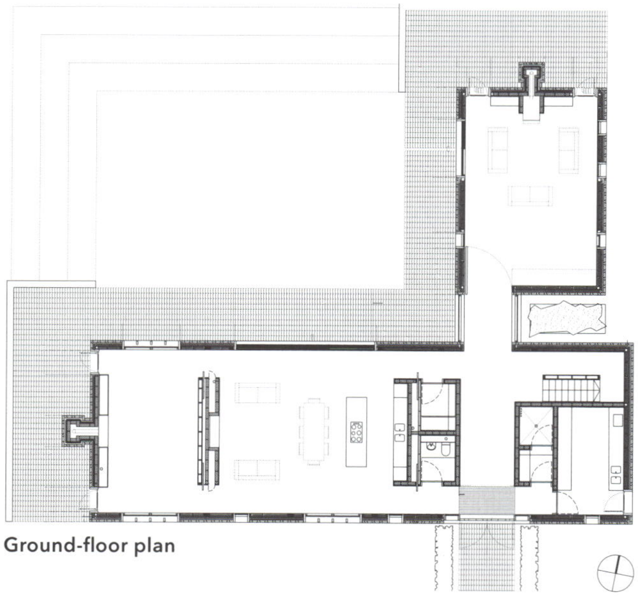

Ground-floor plan

Ström Architects

THE QUEST

This new-build home replaced an ageing bungalow, which had been on the site since 1917. The clients wanted a house for retirement; one that demonstrated their keen interest in design and love of abstract and modern art but eschewed the usual trappings of staid retirement home design.

Early in the design process it was established that a single-storey building would suit the retired clients' future needs and the needs of their disabled daughter. An elegant solution to the steeply sloped site allowed for simple arrangements of space. The design also reduced visual impact from across the valley when looking back towards the house. The sloping site and its protected mature trees very much dictated the positioning of the dwelling.

The architects made use of a retaining wall faced in local Purbeck stone to define different levels and visually mask the vehicular route. This maintains a clear view from the living spaces across the valley. The house cantilevers over the retaining wall and creates a sheltered undercroft parking area. The large cantilever has been achieved through two concrete planes: the floor and roof acting together like a space beam. The concrete structure has been in-filled with simple timber dry lining, leaving the concrete frame externally visible.

Internally, a large open-plan kitchen/dining/living area occupies the centre of the plan, with a covered terrace spanning its length and providing a sheltered outdoor area overlooking southern views. To the Eastern end of the house are the guest accommodation and studies, with the master suite located within the cantilevered western end of the house.

A simple interior palette of Purbeck stone flooring, a concrete hearth and engineered timber flooring provide echoes of the external materials – waterproof concrete slabs and untreated larch cladding.

The house exemplifies the belief that simplicity and honesty of construction underpin good design.

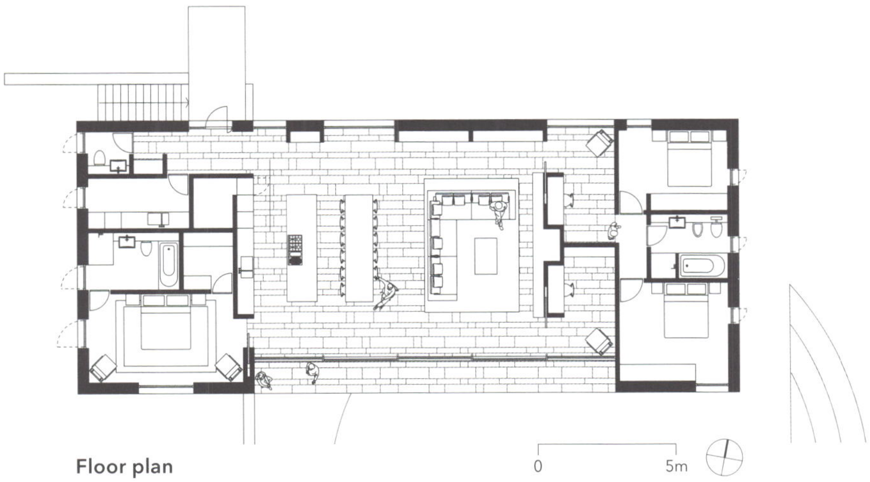

Floor plan

PROJECT SPECIFICATIONS

Location: Swanage, Dorset, England
Area: 205 m^2 (2207 ft^2)
Completed: 2015
Photography: Martin Gardner (pages 199, 200, 201); Michael Sinclair (pages 202, 203)

Rose Garden House borders an architectural conservation area on a granite plateau at the foot of the Dublin Mountains. The home's exposed timber beams and sedum roof allow it to blend with the landscape and sit quietly on the site.

The clients wanted a home that would reflect their personalities and lifestyles whilst feeling rurally idyllic despite its city location. Their extended family live either side of the site and requested that the home blend in with the landscape as much as possible. As a result, the home can barely be seen from the road and is deceptively private.

Triona Stack Architects

ROSE GARDEN HOUSE

The central spinal rooflight brings light and air to the heart of the house, whilst careful passive design maximises solar heat gain. The home's layout tracks the path of the sun. The bedrooms face east to the dawn light, the open-plan kitchen space opens to the southerly gardens, and the living room looks to the setting sun.

Floor plan

Large glass doors open out onto the patio and garden, creating a continuation of play space for the children and a haven of nature for the whole family to explore and enjoy. The south-facing aspect brings light and warmth into the main-living space throughout the seasons. Large brick walls bookend the space and huge wooden beams run across the room, providing great character and age that new builds can sometimes lack.

Built especially for a family with young children, the house allows for both shared times and quiet moments. It has been designed for lifetime living.

PROJECT SPECIFICATIONS

Location: Dublin, Ireland
Area: 300 m^2 (3229 ft^2)
Completed: 2014
Photography: Alice Clancy

Scenario House was purchased with the intention of completely renovating, extending and adapting to the scenarios of the architects' own family life. It presented them with an opportunity to practice their design principles on a more personal level.

The main design challenge was finding a way of physically and visually connecting the front part of the house, originally two separate Victorian reception rooms, with the basement level, which was a full floor height below.

Scenario Architecture

SCENARIO HOUSE

Creating an open, split-level, double reception – connected to the kitchen and garden floor by an angled, glazed-roof extension and a floating library feature leading up the bedroom floors – solved this challenge and created a sense of singular and connected space.

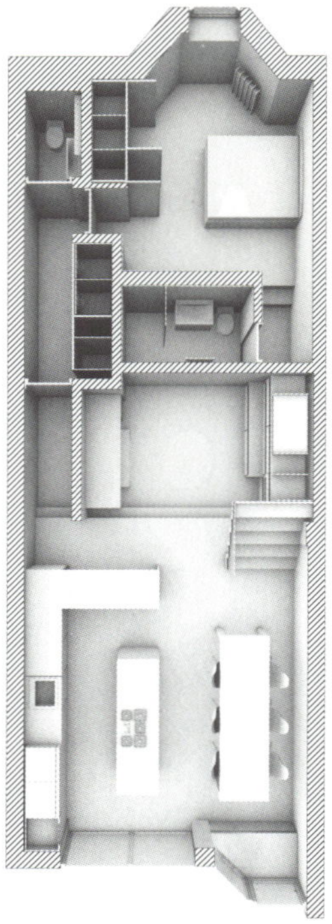

Lower ground-floor plan

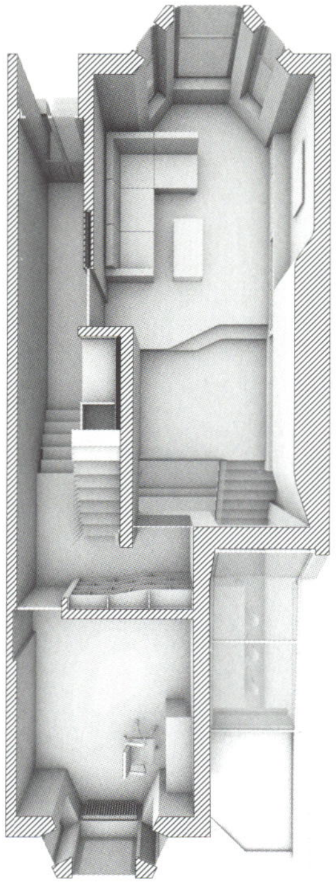

Ground-floor plan

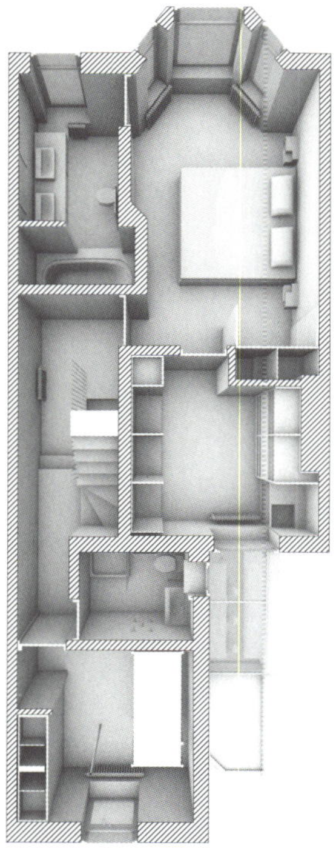

First-floor plan

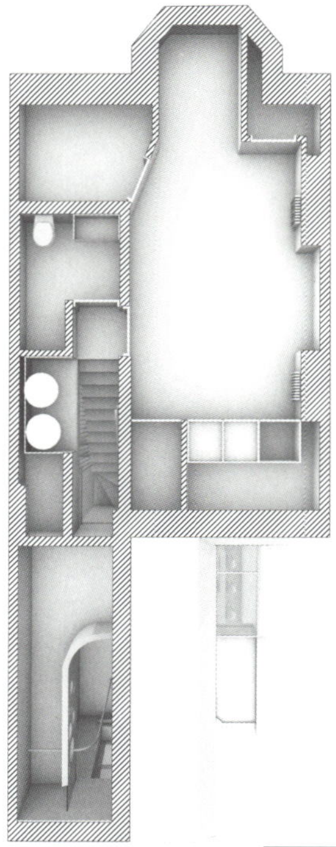

Loft floor plan

0 5m

The design brief was created with consideration for both current and future scenarios, and a conscious effort was made to use every available space the house had to offer. This meant using spaces under the stairs, in the eaves, in hallways, and limited-height areas.

One such space included the relatively low-ceiling height area caused by the lowering of the reception above. This presented an opportunity for a fun and practical children's area. A storage unit under the stairs, complete with a pull-out table and bench, invites the children to spend time playing or doing homework and artwork in a designated but connected part of the home.

PROJECT SPECIFICATIONS

Location: London, England
Area: 220 m^2 (2368 ft^2)
Completed: 2016
Photography: Matt Clayton

The architects' children played a central role in developing both the brief and the design of their own bedroom, which resulted in a climbing wall leading to a secret space at the eaves of the single-pitch original house extension and a fireman's pole.

A contemporary and innovative two-storey house replaces what was an undistinguished 1950s bungalow. The site lies within the Bath and Bristol green belt on the edge of a scattered settlement in Stoney Littleton.

The building sits more or less on the footprint of the earlier building. It incorporates living accommodation on the ground floor and two en suite bedrooms on the first floor. The open-plan kitchen and dining area features full-height glazing, which overlooks the terrace to the fields and views beyond. Solar gain is carefully controlled with heat mirror glazing technology and external blinds, which allow for comfortable room temperatures throughout the year and minimal heating costs. Multiple floor levels break up the living space and create a sense of zone variation within the plan. To the east of the building a book-lined snug is tucked away to one side. To the west lies a single-storey studio filled with light from full-height glazing as well as a bathroom and utility room. Adjacent to the house and its garden is a wild flower meadow.

Andrew Wood Associates and Designscape Architects

SPRINGFIELD FARM

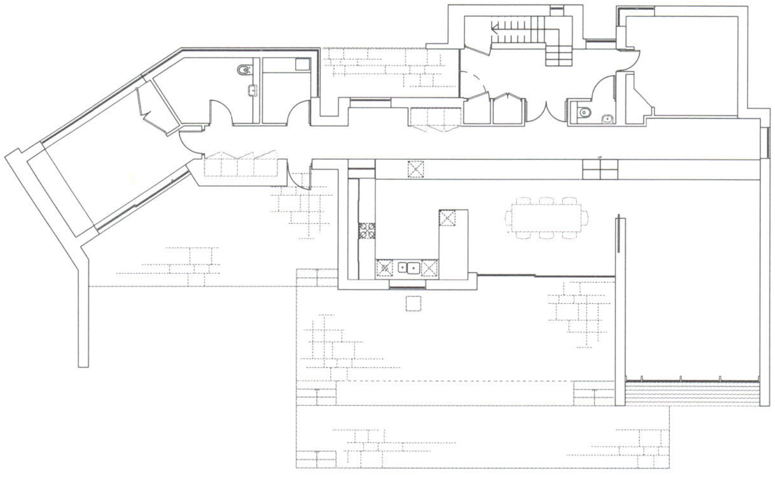

Ground-floor plan

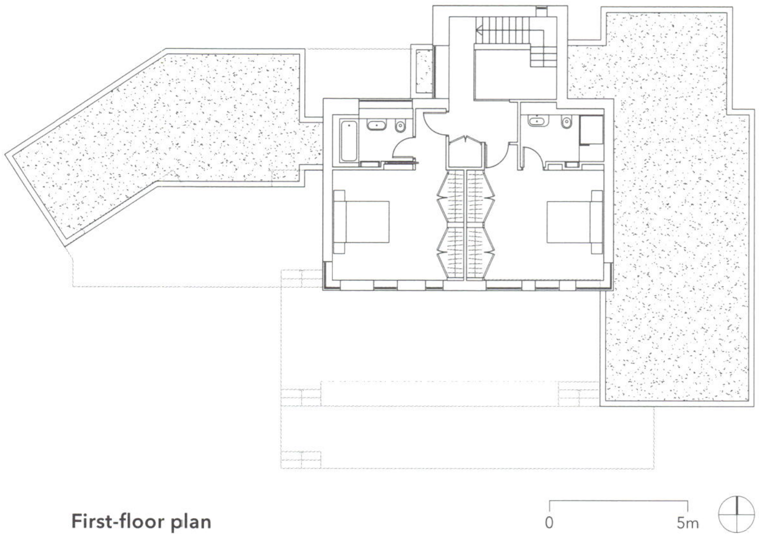

First-floor plan

The design of the building attempts to keep the house as low as possible on the sloping site, whilst simultaneously taking advantage of the attractive views across the Wellow Brook valley.

Natural and sustainable materials have been selected to complement the rural surroundings and colours of buildings in the area. The home's timber frame supports Frake hardwood cladding, which turns silvery grey as it ages and weathers, complementing the grey colours of local Lias limestone. Trespa Mateon cladding panels have been used on the stair tower and within the recesses to express plan articulation, whilst a pale grey Parex render has been used for the studio walls.

The aluminium window frames are a satin finish and coloured to blend with and complement the cladding and grey render. An extensive green roof on the studio is linked to the wild flower meadow by a raised bank. The banks are planted to blend with the adjacent meadow.

PROJECT SPECIFICATIONS

Location: Stoney Littleton, Bath, England
Area: 259 m² (2788 ft²)
Completed: 2014
Photography: Mark Bolton

This project converted and redesigned a 1950s St John Ambulance station into a four-bedroom family retreat and creative workspace within the ancient citadel of Rye, in East Sussex.

The former St John Ambulance station was located within a private walled courtyard, which it shared with a Grade II–listed Georgian house.

Marta Nowicka – DOM stay and live

ST JOHN – RYE

After purchasing the property in 2013, the interior architect was challenged to create a space that would suit the aspirant lifestyle of Rye whilst also capturing its medieval history and the station's industrial past. By keeping the original lofty ground-floor area as living and working space and creating cosy bedrooms upstairs accessed via a large hallway, the brief was successfully implemented.

Removing a central wall and returning the station to its original floor plan created a large 72.5-square-metre (780-square-foot) open-plan living space on the ground floor. In keeping with the historical surroundings, the scheme of the design evokes medieval nuances with exposed-roof timber purlins and a central hearth from which the living space emanates. A double-sided wood burner sits within the vast entertaining space surrounding the hearth. A large concrete plinth cast at the centre divides the space into different zones. This medieval tone has been mixed with medical references, such as a stainless-steel nurses' trolley. The trolley has been used in the upstairs bathroom as a washstand/vanity unit with a large basin and mirror. The original ambulance doors were remade into an art piece and now feature in the living space.

The overall style of the home is minimalistic with a mixture of textured materials, which add warmth. Original exposed brickwork and wide engineered oak flooring runs throughout the ground and first floors and continues to clad the walls of the double-height stairwell and bedrooms in the roof space. In the living space, a wrought ironwork light-fitting feature hangs over a large dining table made of reclaimed beach timber rescued from Camber Sands. The brushed stainless-steel kitchen island references the medical industry and complements the sandblasted, greyed-timber cabinets and stunning Carrera marble worktops and splashbacks.

PARKING BY
PERMIT ONLY

The 1970s side extension was rebuilt. Drawing from modern local vernacular architectural inspirations, the new clad exterior of the extension – constructed with local Lydd handmade clay-peg tiles – fuses well with the existing roof-peg tiles and red-brick building, creating a unified and site-specific look. The surrounding listed garden brick walls influenced the door and window positioning. Bespoke architectural glass windows provide ample natural light and breathtaking rooftop and countryside views.

PROJECT SPECIFICATIONS

Location: Rye, East Sussex, England
Area: 215 m^2 (2314 ft^2)
Completed: 2015
Photography: Voytek Ketz/Vision and Photography

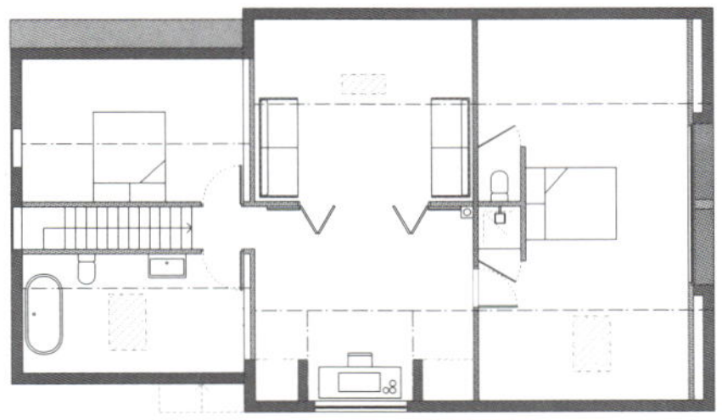

First-floor plan

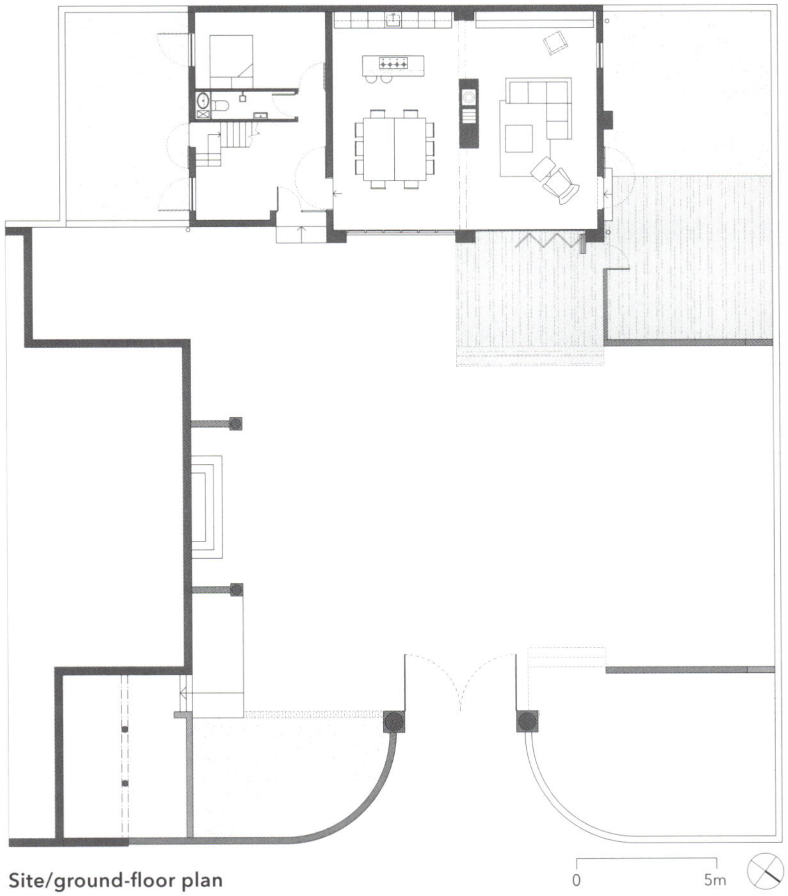

Site/ground-floor plan

re|form [architects + urban strategists]

THE THATCHED COTTAGE

Prior to the owners purchasing the house, the original cottage had been extended with a traditional brick and thatch component. The old extension created space in the new project for an updated kitchen and cloakroom facility, with bathroom and bedroom/study above.

The previous renovation, whilst providing nicely proportioned internal spaces, had failed to connect the house with the garden, so a more open and inclusive solution was sought. The aim of the project was to create a completely new space whilst utilising the massing of the previous extension and honouring the building's historic nature.

The bold move was taken to relocate the kitchen from its previous location into the new extension and free up the previous kitchen space to provide for a snug, which was better suited to an enclosed area of the house. This also achieved the desired link between the kitchen and external environment, allowing the client to feel connected to the garden even on days of inclement weather.

The design exploits the change of level across the garden to its advantage, recessing the room into the ground when viewed from the approach, which helps to reduce its impact upon the original property.

PROJECT SPECIFICATIONS

Location: Cheshire, England

Area: 138 m² (1485 ft²)

Completed: 2015

Photography: Kitchen Architecture

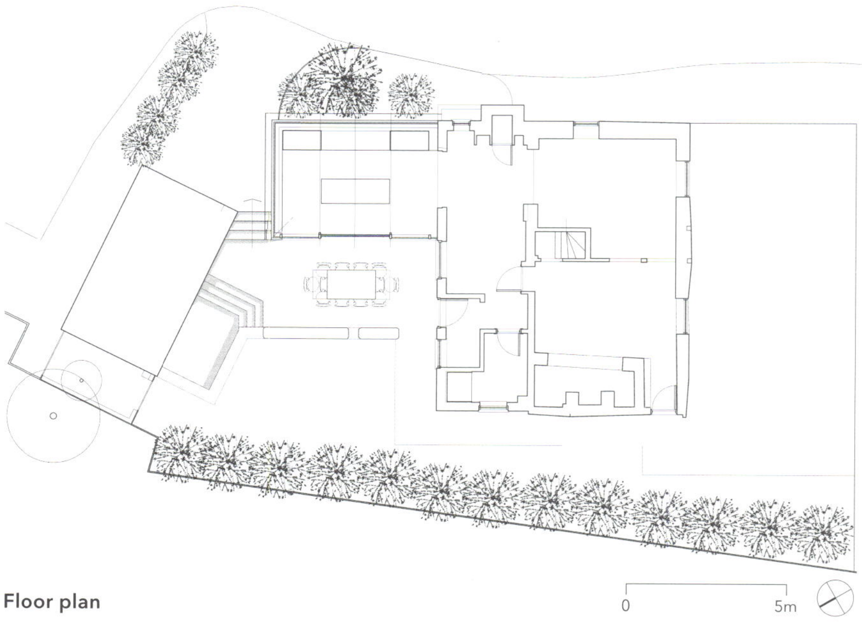

Floor plan

Materials and detailing were chosen to complement the existing house. The stone-flagged flooring provides continuity between the inside and the outside spaces, and the glazed walls of the new space are chased in to the existing brickwork, allowing the older structure to be read visually behind the new. Structural framing was kept to a minimum and used not only as a means of support to the glazed panels but also as a means of distributing services, power and lighting. The Bulthaup kitchen complements the simplicity of the space and was chosen for its bold form and minimal detailing. The client's own collection of classic furniture pieces add a touch of personal occupancy and warmth to the finished home.

Broadstone Architects

TIREIGHTER CAIRN

A rich cultural and natural environment influenced the design of this family dwelling in rural County Derry/Londonderry. Located on the periphery of Park Village, the land is surrounded by panoramic views of the Sperrin Mountains and is adjacent to a neolithic wedge tomb. Located further along Tireighter Road is a clachan displaying traditional characteristics of rural settlement, such as limewashed gables and boundary walls.

Three distinct but inter-connecting blocks make up the home's form. The blocks were designed to convey a nearby burial chamber entrance and its three primary standing stones.

Similar to the clachan, each building bears a relationship with the other through proportional increases in scale, whilst clustered buildings step down the site via central circulation.

In this regard, the home replicates a local Palladian styled dwelling, in particular, Tamnagh Lodge, which prompted the design reference to Palladian villas and how a centrally lit entrance hall and circulation might work in accessing bedrooms and living/kitchen areas on upper, middle and lower floor plates.

Two of the three central entrance stacks act as both internal and external lightwells, whilst the third is a chimney for the living room stove. The two stairwells within the connecting spaces between the blocks allow for vistas from the entrance hall to the surrounding landscape and mountain range.

The materiality of the home makes reference to the wedge tomb's dense massing, the thick white gable walls of the clachan and the tall chimneys of Tamnagh Lodge. Building orientation, similar to the wedge-shaped tomb, provides a blank north façade with extending walls for privacy.

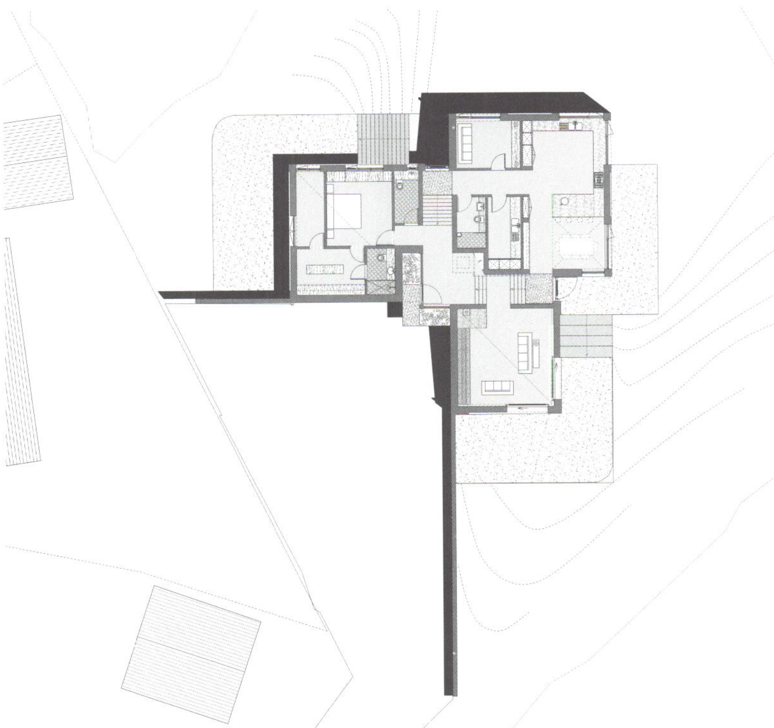

Ground-floor plan

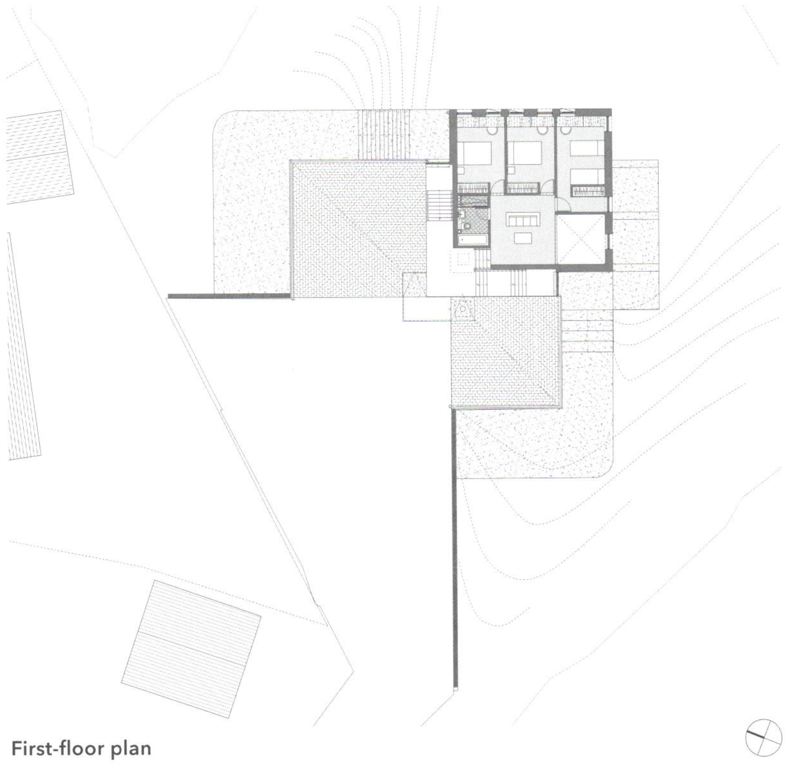

First-floor plan

PROJECT SPECIFICATIONS

Location: County Derry/Londonderry, Northern Ireland
Area: 250 m² (2691 ft²)
Completed: 2016
Photography: Aidan Monaghan

Deteriorated and out of use for over 40 years, the existing single-storey workshop was demolished to expose an angled site. Surrounded on three sides by adjoining buildings and within a tightly held conservation area, the architects had to overcome numerous site challenges associated with density, rights to light, and planning stipulations on height. The result is a two-bedroom terrace built over three storeys.

Kirkwood McCarthy

WINKLEY WORKSHOP

Though humble to the street, the project is a voluminous residence referential to its setting yet of its own time. Stacked floor plates establish a natural zoning diagram within the property that transitions from the public/living basement floor to the private/sleeping first floor. Existing brickwork features, folded metal stairs and softened walnut floors articulate this program.

20

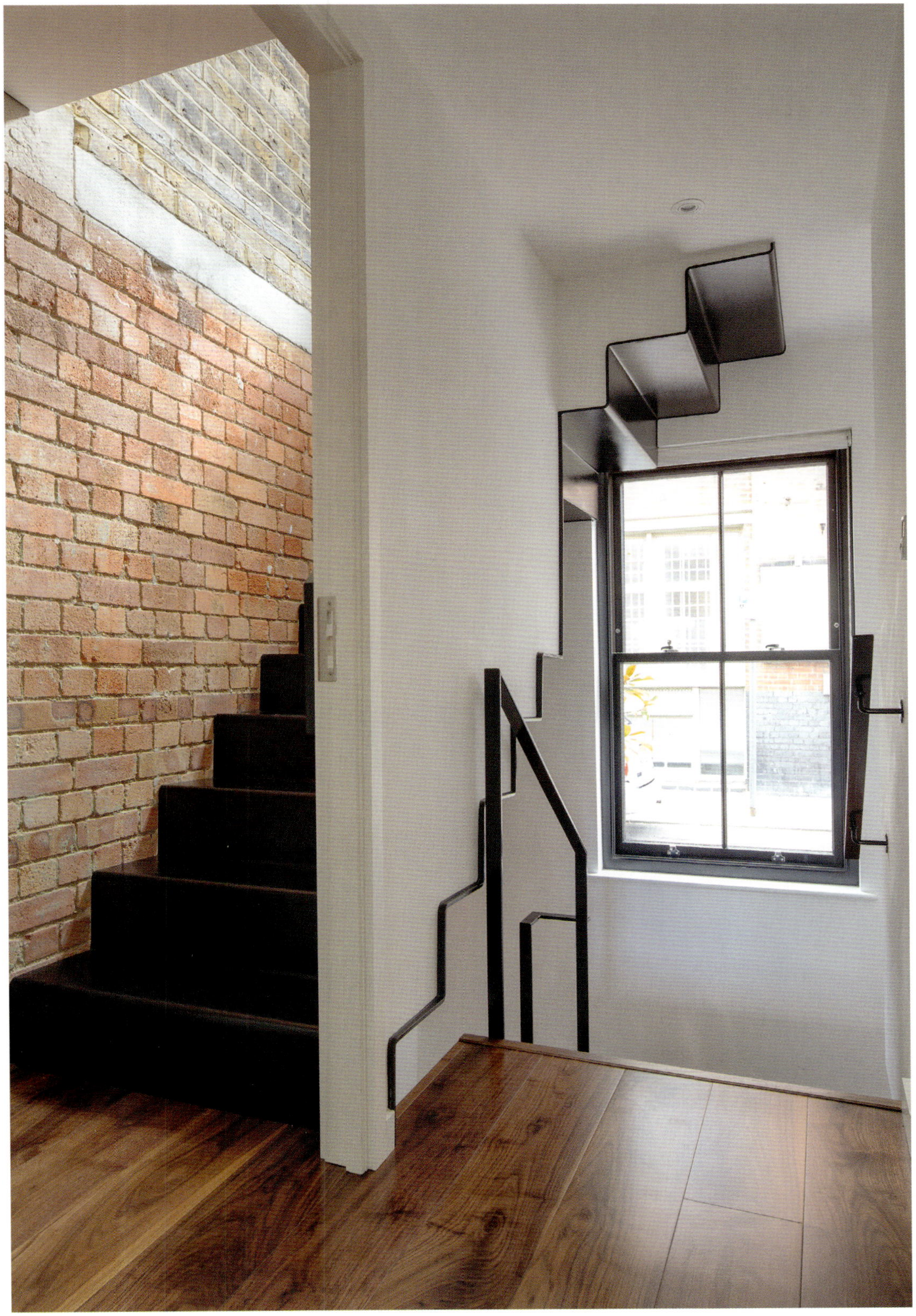

The home is entered via the street onto a split-level landing, which connects the basement with an upper-ground floor. This landing level, with perforated folded-steel stair, allows light from the southern street window to fall deep into the basement. This casts a gentle circular pattern on the brick basement floor below and forges a visual connection between the entrance and living area.

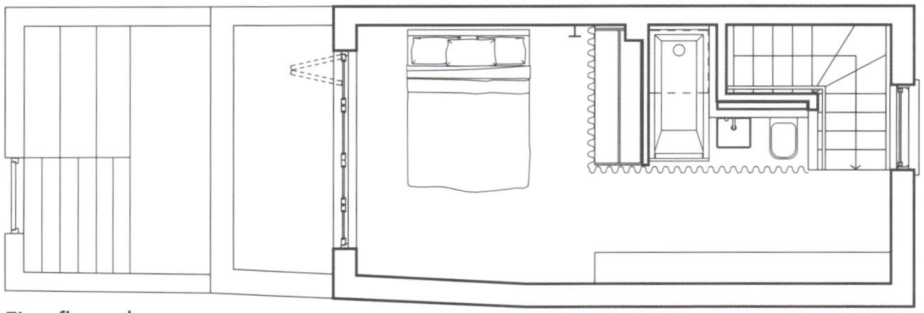

First-floor plan

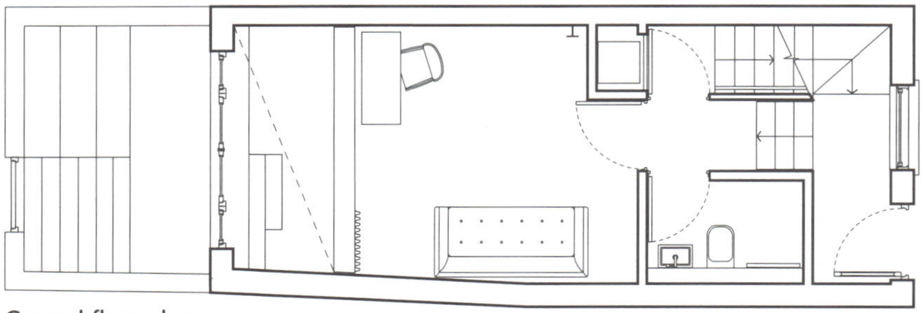

Ground-floor plan

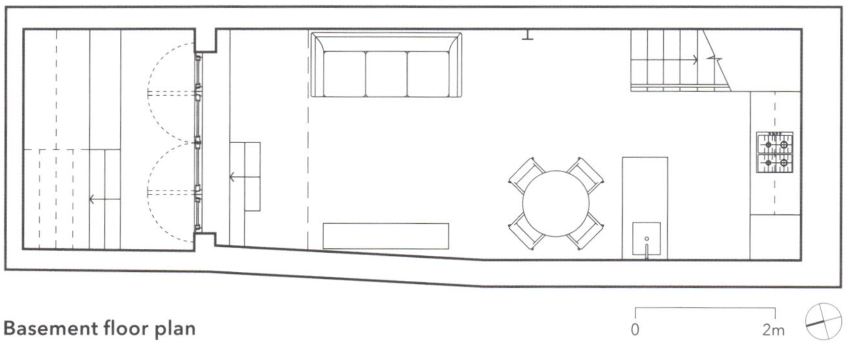

Basement floor plan

Open-plan living, dining and kitchen areas lead out onto the courtyard space at basement level. Soaring double-height glazing maximises internal daylight levels and sky views. It also integrates the living and outdoors spaces. The basement floor is covered with a herringbone-laid brick paver, which continues through to the courtyard, making the spaces feel like one shared indoor/outdoor experience. The basement-floor level steps up to the courtyard, and up again to the ground level of Teesdale Yard at the rear of the site.

SMLXL

PROJECT SPECIFICATIONS

Location: London, England
Area: 68 m^2 (732 ft^2)
Completed: 2014
Photography: David Butler

At the upper-ground floor a flexible mezzanine bedroom/study space is divided by a bookcase and curtain from the living area and courtyard below. A private master bedroom with en suite and balcony occupies the top floor.

Externally, bricks localise the building within its setting. Internally, the palette is simple and continuous. The basement and courtyard are paved with herringbone bricks, which forge continuity between indoor and outdoor living spaces. A walnut stair with built-in cupboards leads from the basement to the ground floor and walnut flooring continues to the upper two storeys to distinguish bedroom spaces. Black folded-steel stairs punctuate circulation between the ground and first floors. The ground-floor metal stair is perforated to allow a passage of sunlight to enter the basement level, and the first-floor metal stair is enclosed with a suspended stud wall to provide an acoustic barrier to the master bedroom. The rest of the house has a simple and controlled material palette: white walls exaggerate light and space; black detailing highlights the journey through the house; and curtains for flexible privacy provide a softening element.

Graham Smith Making

Located in New Forest National Park, this private dwelling was designed as a two-storey replacement for a 1930s bungalow. The site sits amongst fields and woodland just outside the park, with a heavily treed and well-established garden.

The clients wanted a comfortable and contemporary home as a weekend house, one that would eventually become their future permanent home. With busy lives in London, they needed a weekend retreat to relax and entertain friends. As keen gardeners and

Ström Architects

WOODPECKERS

outdoor lifestyle enthusiasts, a strong relationship with the garden as well as the surrounding countryside was an important design factor. Both involved in the design world, their aspirations for built and aesthetic qualities were high; they wanted a house that would be simple but elegant – stylish rather than fashionable.

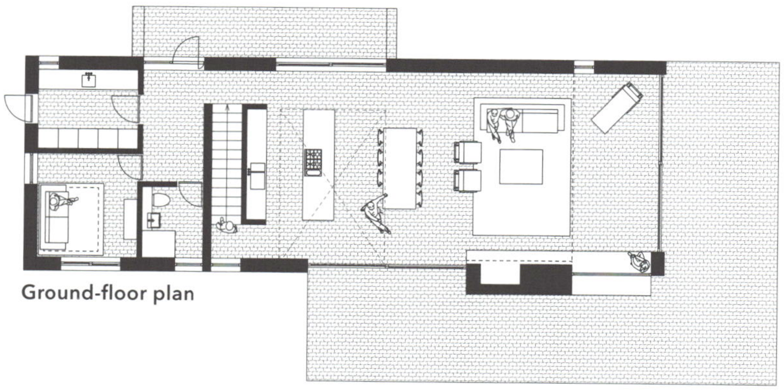

Ground-floor plan

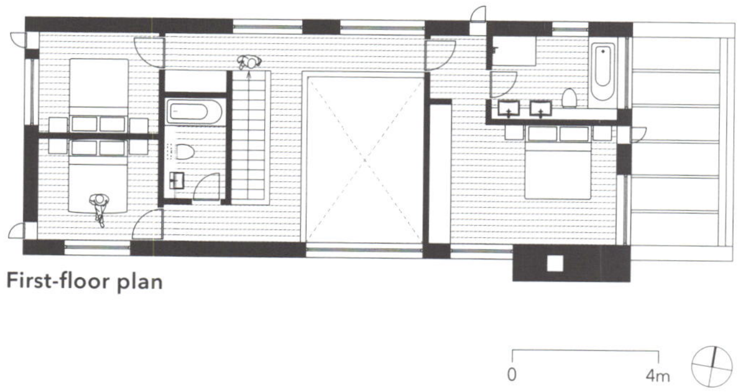

First-floor plan

To create a strong internal-external relationship, traditional masonry to create large openings would be required, ultimately attracting costs and diluting the simplicity of a singular structural strategy. As it stands, the structure is entirely timber studwork and sits on a piled concrete slab. The studwork is filled and over-clad with insulation, creating a thermally and structurally efficient envelope. Planning constraints dictated that floor area could only be increased by 30 percent, with an additional 20 square metres (215 square feet) for a conservatory. Due to these restrictions it was established that a slab-sided volume would be best suited, pushing glazing to the outer edge of the envelope. By integrating a single-storey, almost flat-roofed element, which continues out seamlessly from the main open-plan space, the architects were able to avoid the typical aesthetic of a domestic conservatory.

The clients have ended up spending more time at the house than initially expected – long weekends, weeks spent working from home and extended stays hosting family during holidays – making Woodpeckers much more than a weekend getaway.

PROJECT SPECIFICATIONS

Location: New Forest National Park, England
Area: 195 m^2 (2099 ft^2)
Completed: 2015
Photography: Luke Hayes

INDEX OF ARCHITECTS